EARTH'S FINAL MOMENTS

JOHN HAGEE

CHARISMA
HOUSE

Most Charisma House Book Group products are available at special quantity discounts for bulk purchase for sales promotions, premiums, fund-raising, and educational needs. For details, write Charisma House Book Group, 600 Rinehart Road, Lake Mary, Florida 32746, or telephone (407) 333-0600.

Earth's Final Moments by John Hagee
Published by Charisma House
Charisma Media/Charisma House Book Group
600 Rinehart Road
Lake Mary, Florida 32746
www.charismahouse.com

Visit the author's website at www.jhm.org.

Library of Congress Cataloging-in-Publication Data:

Hagee, John.
  Earth's final moments / John Hagee.
      p. cm.
  Includes bibliographical references (p.   ).
  ISBN 978-1-61638-487-6 (casebound) -- ISBN 978-1-61638-574-3
(e-book)
-- ISBN 978-1-61638-596-5 (international trade pbk.) 1.
Bible--Prophecies--Armageddon. 2. Bible--Prophecies--Middle
East. I.
Title.
  BS649.A68H34 2011
  236'.9--dc23

                              2011025495

Portions of this book were previously published as *Jerusalem
Countdown* by FrontLine, copyright © 2006, 2007, ISBN
978-1-59979-089-3.

11 12 13 14 15 — 987654321
Printed in the United States of America

Contents

IMPENDING DOOM

EARTH IS CAREENING toward its final act—are you prepared?

In this small book about Earth's final moments, we will take a look at some powerful insights about the prophetic signs in Scripture that are intersecting with our lives in the twenty-first century today. When will the world end? How will it end? The Scriptures are not silent about the future of our world and the events leading to the end of the age. In response to their request for a "sign of Your coming," in Matthew 24, Jesus gave His twelve disciples the spine of prophecy as they sat on the Mount of Olives overlooking the beautiful city of Jerusalem:

> Now as He sat on the Mount of Olives, the disciples came to Him privately, saying, "Tell us...what

will be the sign of Your coming, and of the end of the age?" And Jesus answered and said to them: "Take heed that no one deceives you. For many will come in My name, saying, 'I am the Christ,' and will deceive many. And you will hear of wars and rumors of wars. See that you are not troubled; for all these things must come to pass, but the end is not yet. For nation will rise against nation, and kingdom against kingdom. And there will be famines, pestilences, and earthquakes in various places. All these are the beginning of sorrows. Then they will deliver you up to tribulation and kill you, and you will be hated by all nations for My name's sake. And then many will be offended, will betray one another, and will hate one another. Then many false prophets will rise up and deceive many. And because lawlessness will abound, the love of many will grow cold. But he who endures to the end shall be saved."

—MATTHEW 24:3–13

There are many prophetic signs in Scripture that describe the world in the last days. When all of these ten prophetic signs begin to occur in one generation, that generation will see the end of the age. To begin our look at Earth's final moments, I am including a short listing of ten signs that will be fulfilled in one short generational span at the beginning of Earth's final season. As you read this list, consider carefully the climate and circumstances of this present age.

Ten Prophetic Signs of the End Time World
1. The knowledge explosion—Daniel 12:4
2. Plague in the Middle East—Zechariah 14:12–15
3. The rebirth of Israel—Isaiah 66:8–10
4. The Jews will return home—Jeremiah 23:7–8
5. Jerusalem no longer under Gentile control—Luke 21:24
6. International and instant communication—Revelation 11:3, 7–10
7. Days of deception—Matthew 24:4
8. Famines and pestilence—Matthew 24:7–8
9. Earthquakes—Matthew 24:7–8
10. "As in the days of Noah…"—Matthew 24:36–39

EARTH'S FINAL MOMENTS BEGIN WITH THE JEWS

The beginning of Earth's final moments leads back to Genesis 17, where God established an everlasting covenant with the father of God's chosen people, Abraham. As an old man of ninety-nine years, Abram was visited by God and given the honor of establishing a covenant with God Himself, one resulting with his descendants—God's chosen people—inheriting the land of Canaan.

God did more than change Abram's name to Abraham in that visitation—He changed the course of history for all time. God told Abraham:

> As for Me, behold, My covenant is with you, and you shall be a father of many nations....I will establish My covenant between Me and you and your descendants after you in their generations, for an everlasting covenant, to be God to you and your descendants after you. Also I give to you and your descendants after you the land in which you are a stranger, all the land of Canaan, as an everlasting possession; and I will be their God.
>
> —GENESIS 17:4, 7–8

But God's covenant with Abraham and His chosen people carried responsibility as well as blessing for the Jews. The point is clearly established in the Bible that *Israel's response* to the blessing of the gift of the Promised Land determined *God's response* to them. At the time of the dedication of Solomon's temple, when God's presence came down and took up residence in that holy place, God warned His people with these words:

> If you turn away and forsake My statutes and My commandments which I have set before you, and go and serve other gods, and worship them, then I

will uproot them [the Jews] from My land which I have given them; and this house [temple], which I have sanctified for My name I will cast out of My sight, and will make it a proverb and a byword among all peoples.

—2 CHRONICLES 7:19–20

It was the disobedience and rebellion of the Jews, God's chosen people, to their covenantal responsibility to serve only the one true God, Jehovah, that gave rise to the opposition and persecution they experienced beginning in Canaan and continuing to this very day. In no way does this lessen or excuse the mistreatment and sinful atrocities the Jews have endured at the hands of their enemies, but it gives us a framework for understanding what leads up to Earth's final moments.

The words of God in the verses above were a warning. The verses that follow are no warning—they are the execution of judgment from God Himself for the disobedience of His people:

Because they have forsaken My law which I set before them, and have not obeyed My voice, nor walked according to it, but they have walked according to the dictates of their own hearts and after the Baals...I will scatter them also among the Gentiles.

—Jeremiah 9:13–16

How utterly repulsive, insulting, and heartbreaking to God for His chosen people to turn to idols instead of remaining faithful to Him so they would obtain the blessings He would shower upon His faithful chosen people. Their own rebellion had birthed the seed of anti-Semitism that would arise and bring destruction to them for centuries to come.

As a result of their disobedience, great persecution has befallen the Jews. Some of it happened during the days in which God's Word was being written, long before the term *anti-Semitism* had been voiced by anyone. It has plagued the Jews throughout the ages. Although it rises from the judgment of God upon His rebellious chosen people, it is sin—and it damns the soul. Where it raises its ugly head today, it must be eradicated, and repentance must flow where condemnation has prevailed.

History reveals humanity's triumphs and failures, giving us a compass for the future. Jerusalem has been a strategic site in the Middle East for three thousand years. The sacred city has been the object of numerous attacks and sieges. Perched on easily defensible Judean hillsides less than thirty miles from the Mediterranean Sea,

Jerusalem controlled the major highways that connected Egypt, Europe, and Africa. Therefore, whoever controlled Jerusalem had the ability to control the Middle East, economically and militarily. In addition to its military significance, the spiritual importance of Jerusalem to the Jews, Christians, and Muslims has made it the object of wars to gain possession of the city like no other city in the world.

Those wars are not over. The greatest war the world has ever seen will soon envelop Israel and Jerusalem. It will come at the conclusion of Earth's final moments.

How Does This Affect You?

If September 11 proved anything, it proved America is not immune from attack from our enemies. September 11 also proved, beyond any reasonable doubt, that our enemies are willing to use whatever weapons they have to kill as many of us as possible. The highest honor in Islam is to die as a martyr killing Christians and Jews. The one who does this awakes in an Islamic heaven surrounded by seventy-two virgins.

The UN will send their nuclear teams to Iran and look the other way as long as possible. Why? Because the UN deeply resents the United States for not bowing to its global agenda. The UN was livid with the Bush administration for going to war in Iraq when the United Nations disapproved of that war. America's invasion of Iraq exposed the corruption in the UN with the "food for oil" scam involving the upper echelon of UN leadership.

If Israel attacks Iran, there doubtless will be a vast pan-Arabic Islamic army assembled to attack Israel and attempt to drive the Jews into the Dead Sea. Once again, Jerusalem becomes the target! In recent days, a danger with consequences just as catastrophic to Israel has begun—the rise of violence in Egypt. A casual glance at the geopolitical crisis of the Middle East with rogue terrorist states in possession of nuclear weapons makes one thing clear—we are standing on the brink of a nuclear Armageddon.

No prophetic scripture is more crystal clear than Ezekiel's vivid and specific description of the coming massive war in the Middle East that will sweep the world toward Armageddon. Ezekiel's war as described in chapters 38 and 39 will consist of an Arab coalition of nations led by Russia for the purpose of exterminating the Jews of Israel and controlling the city of Jerusalem. The Russian payout will be the ability to control the oil-rich Persian Gulf.

What will be Iran's response to Israel's military attack

of their nuclear weapons' plants? How will Syria, Saudi Arabia, Jordan, Egypt, and Libya respond?

If these Arab nations unite their forces under Russia's leadership, which has been helping Iran develop nuclear weapons for several years, the inferno described in Ezekiel 38–39 will explode across the Middle East, plunging the world toward Armageddon.

Iran's president seems to be escalating the confrontation of Iran's Islamic hard-line factions and policies with Israel's determination for continued self-government and independence. Iran has indicated that it will never again suspend conversion of uranium ore and has openly shown not only its determination to develop a bomb but also the testing of the first bomb with nuclear capacity.

What would a confrontation with the Middle East look like for America? What would happen if America entered the battle zone in defense of Israel? What does the future look like between the Middle East and America? These are questions in the minds of many Americans today, and in this book we will consider some of the possible answers to these questions and others.

When we finish, we will have a clearer vision of what Earth's final moments will look like—not just for Israel but also for the entire world, including America.

CHAPTER 1

"CAN THESE BONES LIVE?"

GOD'S CHOSEN PEOPLE, the Jews, and the Promised Land of Israel are the hub that forms the wheel of prophecy. All End Time prophecy focuses first and foremost on Israel's importance to God and His eternal covenant with His chosen people to "give to you and your descendants after you the land in which you are a stranger, all the land of Canaan, as an everlasting possession; and I will be their God" (Gen. 17:8). But because of the Jews' disobedience and rebellion, they were scattered around the globe, and control of their Promised Land of Israel slipped right out of their fingers for hundreds of years.

More than twenty-six hundred years ago the prophet Ezekiel prophesied the resurrection of Israel from the Gentile graves in the lands to which she had been scattered, predicting the rebirth of Israel, which took place on May 14, 1948. Ezekiel also prophesied about the holy war that will take place in Israel some time after Israel's restoration to independence.

God gave Ezekiel a vision of a valley full of dry bones. I want to make it very clear that I do not believe that Ezekiel's vision has anything to do with the resurrection of the dead saints of the church. In Ezekiel 37:11, God told Ezekiel, "Son of man, these bones are the whole house of Israel." There is no doubt in the text this could only be Israel.

In a vision, God took Ezekiel to a valley full of dead bones that were very dry and scattered. This was God's physical portrayal of the nation of Israel. Israel ceased to be a nation in A.D. 70 when the Jews were scattered to the ends of the earth by the Roman army under Titus. It would be more than two thousand years before Israel became a recognized state again in May 1948—and the bones grew very dry!

God asked Ezekiel a perplexing question:

> And He said to me, "Son of man, can these bones live?"
>
> —EZEKIEL 37:3

Ezekiel responded to God by saying, "O Lord God, You know" (v. 3). In other words, he was saying, "I don't see how it's possible. Death has done its work. Life is gone. Lord, if these bones live, it will require the miracle-working power of Jehovah God."

For nearly fifty years I have preached the gospel of Jesus Christ to audiences all over the earth. I have stood in churches, cathedrals, auditoriums, football stadiums, and a preaching field in Nigeria with more than three million people attending. Yet, like Ezekiel, often as I looked over the audiences large and small, I have thought, "Can these bones live?"

In response to Ezekiel's question, God told him to do something very strange. It was the strangest message to the deadest congregation in the history of preaching! God told him to preach the Word of the Lord to the dry bones. "Again He said to me, 'Prophesy to these bones, and say to them, "O dry bones, hear the word of the Lord!"'" (v. 4).

The word *prophesy* doesn't always mean to foretell or to predict. Here it means to speak out or to preach a message to the people of God. There is supernatural power in the spoken Word of God.

Ezekiel's faith conquered the limitations of his carnal mind, and he obeyed the voice of God. It is a Bible fact:

obedience brings blessing, and disobedience brings judgment. Ezekiel looked at the valley full of scattered, very dry bones and preached this message:

> Thus says the Lord GOD to these bones: "Surely I will cause breath to enter into you, and you shall live. I will put sinews on you and bring flesh upon you, cover you with skin and put breath in you; and you shall live. Then you shall know that I am the LORD."
>
> —EZEKIEL 37:5–6

Ezekiel proclaimed that God was going to do a supernatural work that would make those dry, lifeless, scattered bones live again. It would be a reversal of death and corruption.

In perfect obedience to the word of God, Ezekiel said:

> So I prophesied as I was commanded; and as I prophesied, there was a noise, and suddenly a rattling; and the bones came together, bone to bone. Indeed, as I looked, the sinews and the flesh came upon them, and the skin covered them over; but there was no breath in them.
>
> —EZEKIEL 37:7–8

Notice that the restoration to life for the bones was a process. It was not an instantaneous event. The bones were dry, scattered, and dead for a very long time. The dry bones in Ezekiel's vision represent the nation of Israel during the Diaspora, beginning in A.D. 70 (Ezek. 37:11). Gradually the bones came together, and the sinews and flesh came upon them.

It was at this point of Israel's gradual restoration that people like Theodor Herzl, the father of Zionism, began to call the Jews back to Israel. The "sinews and flesh" continued to come together as the Jews of the earth returned to *Eretz*, Israel, to drain the swamps and transform the desert into a rose. On May 14, 1948, at 4:32 p.m., the State of Israel, after two thousand years, was reborn. Ezekiel's prophetic vision was fulfilled:

> Then say to them, "Thus says the Lord God: 'Surely I will take the children of Israel from among the nations, wherever they have gone, and will gather them from every side and bring them into their own land.'"
>
> —EZEKIEL 37:21

God made it exceedingly clear that He would bring the Jews back to *"their own land."* He would not bring them back to the Palestinians' land—He would restore them to the Promised Land of the eternal covenant God had made with Abraham, Isaac, Jacob, and their descendants.

At the conclusion of Ezekiel 37, the nation of Israel had been physically reborn. Today they have a flag; they have a constitution; they have a prime minister and a Knesset. They have a police force, a powerful military might, and the world's best intelligence agencies. They have Jerusalem, the City of God. They have a nation. They have everything but spiritual life.

Like the dry bones of Ezekiel 37, Israel awaits the spiritual awakening of the breath of God and the coming of Messiah.

The Process of Regathering

Prophecy tells us not only what will happen in the future but also the process by which it will happen. The prophet Jeremiah provides us with a series of word pictures illustrating the process by which God would regather Israel.

In Jeremiah 16, the prophet proclaims what has come to be known in our generation as *Exodus II*. Jeremiah declares that Exodus II will completely overshadow the original exodus of Israel from Egypt under Moses's leadership at the original Passover.

"Therefore behold, the days are coming," declares the LORD, "that it shall no more be said, 'The LORD lives who brought up the children of Israel from the land of Egypt,' but, 'The LORD lives who brought up the children of Israel from the land of the north and from all the lands where He had driven them.' For I will bring them back into their land which I gave to their fathers."

—JEREMIAH 16:14–15

This amazing prophecy came from the pen of one of Israel's acknowledged major prophets. For more than three thousand years the Jews celebrated the exodus of Moses from Egypt's bondage as the greatest event in their history. Yet Jeremiah declares there is coming a second exodus that will be so great that the first exodus will pale by comparison.

Jeremiah states that the people will come from "the land of the north," which I believe is Russia. In the Bible, all directions are given from Jerusalem. In the mind of God, Jerusalem is the center of the universe.

Jeremiah expanded his prophecy of Exodus II to include "all the lands where He had driven them." As I write this book, the chief rabbi of Israel has his representatives going to the four corners of the earth to help Jewish people return to Zion. Exodus II is far from complete, as the mighty right hand of God continues to gather "the apple of His eye" to the land given to Abraham and his seed almost six thousand years ago.

Fishers and hunters

The Bible is a book of parables and word pictures describing principles of truth from God to man. The prophet Jeremiah puts his pen to parchment and paints a vivid picture of the human agents God intended to use to bring the Jewish people back to Israel.

> "But now I will send for many fishermen" declares the LORD, "and they will catch them. After that I will send for many hunters, and they will hunt them down on every mountain and hill and from the crevices of the rocks."
>
> —JEREMIAH 16:16, NIV

I believe this verse indicates that the positive comes before the negative. Grace and mercy come before judgment. The fishermen come before the hunters. First, God sent the fishermen to Israel. These were the Zionists, men like Theodor Herzl who called for the Jews of Europe and the world to come to Palestine to establish the Jewish state. The Jews were encouraged to escape while there was still time. The situation for Jews in Europe would only get worse, not better.

A *fisherman* is one who draws his target toward him with bait. Herzl and his fellow Zionists were God's fishermen, calling the sons and daughters of Abraham home. Herzl was deeply disappointed that the Jews of the world did not respond in greater numbers.

God then sent the hunters. The *hunter* is one who pursues his target with force and fear. No one could see the horror of the Holocaust coming, but the force and fear of Hitler's Nazis drove the Jewish people back to the only home God ever intended for the Jews to have—Israel. I stand amazed at the accuracy of God's Word and its relevance for our time. I am stricken with awe and wonder at His boundless love for Israel and the Jewish people and His divine determination that the promise He gave Abraham, Isaac, and Jacob become reality.

"Go to the potter's house."

In Jeremiah 18, the prophet presents a second vivid picture of the process God will use to bring Israel to its divine destiny. God tells Jeremiah to go down to the potter's house, and God declares that He Himself will be the potter.

"Arise and go down to the potter's house."...Then I went down to the potter's house, and there he was, making something at the wheel. And the vessel that he made of clay was marred in the hand of the potter; so he made it again into another vessel, as it seemed good to the potter to make. Then the word of the Lord came to me, saying: "O house of Israel, can I not do with you as this potter?" says the Lord. "Look, as the clay is in the potter's hand, so are you in My hand, O house of Israel!"

—JEREMIAH 18:2–6

God makes it absolutely clear that He is the potter, and the pot in His hand is the nation of Israel. The first time the Lord set out to mold Israel as a potter molds the clay, He envisioned that the clay pot was marred in His hand.

God did not cast the pot away. Instead He crushed the clay on the wheel and formed it into a second pot, whereby the divine destiny of the Jewish people could be realized according to His eternal plan.

On one of my many trips to Israel, I was taken to a potter's house in Hebron. Here the potter was making pottery on a pottery wheel just as masters of his craft had done for thousands of years before. He took a lump of clay, moistened his hands, and, as he pumped the spinning wheel with his feet, carefully began shaping the clay into the image locked in his mind.

He found lumps and imperfections in the clay and plucked them out, throwing them onto the floor. Patiently, he shaped the pot, and when it didn't come together, he smashed it and began again. The second pot came out perfectly as everyone in our group applauded.

God, the Master Potter, has shaped Israel a second time. The process continues with imperfections being plucked out and cast aside. The pot will reach perfection when Messiah comes, and the whole earth will applaud as Jerusalem becomes the "praise in the earth" (Isa. 62:7).

CHAPTER 2

BIRTH PAINS OF THE NEW AGE

JESUS PRESENTED A portrait of the end of the age and the coming of the Messiah. He presents a series of signs, including international wars, famines, and earthquakes. He makes a profound statement: "All these are the beginning of birth pains" (Matt. 24:8, NIV).

There are two facts about a woman in labor about to have a child. First, when the birth pains start, they do not stop until the child is born. Second, the birth pains become more severe and more rapid as birth approaches. The last pain is the greatest pain, and it is soon forgotten with the birth of the new child.

The world and Israel are now having contractions (wars, rumors of wars, acts of terrorism, bloodshed, and violence around the globe) that will produce a new

Messianic era. The increasing rapidity and intensifying of these birth pains can be seen on the newscasts every evening. We are racing toward the end of the age. Messiah is coming much sooner than you think!

As Ezekiel 37 comes to a close, the prophet mentions two sticks (Ezek. 37:15–28). These two sticks represent the northern (Israel) and southern (Judah) kingdoms, which will again become one nation.

That means there are no "ten lost tribes of Israel," for God never loses anything. Ezekiel writes: "The nations also will know that I, the LORD, sanctify Israel…" (v. 28). God is performing this awesome miracle to testify to the nations of the world of His boundless love for Israel as He sanctifies that nation prior to Messiah's coming.

CONSIDER THE PARADE OF NATIONS AT WAR

Terrorism is affecting many nations of our world. Because of the attacks by Islamic terrorists, there is today a parade of nations who have entered the war with Islam.

America is at war with radical Islam.

America did not respond to the terrorist attacks during the Carter administration when the radical Islamic group led by Ayatollah Khomeini overran the American embassy in Tehran, capturing more than sixty US hostages and demanding an apology from America, whom they considered "the Great Satan." Mobs burned the American flag and shouted, "Death to America," which was seen on national television in America.[1]

By counting the number of days that the hostages had been held in captivity, nightly announcements such as, "America Held Hostage, Day Eighty-Nine," focused on the prolonged aspect of the situation.[2] The American people began to see President Carter as a weak leader, and the hostage crisis led to his political demise. This hostage crisis caused radical Islamics to see America as weak and powerless to stop their terrorist attacks. History supports this fact: weakness breeds war.

America retreated from Beirut, Lebanon, in 1983, when two hundred twenty US Marines were killed by Hezbollah terrorists—the same terrorists who attacked Israel on July 12, 2006, killing eight Israeli soldiers and kidnapping two others, which have yet to be returned.[3]America did nothing!

When the terrorists attacked the New York World Trade Center in 1993 during the Clinton administration, America did nothing![4]

When the US Embassy in Tanzania was attacked in 1998, President Clinton fired missiles into an abandoned terrorist camp, killing several sand dunes and terrifying a few camels. This bold and fearless action was taken to get his sexual exploits with Monica Lewinsky of the front pages of America's newspapers. Again—America did nothing![5]

When the USS *Cole* was attacked by terrorists in 2000, an investigation could not find who was responsible…and America did nothing once again![6]

Then came 9/11. The terrorists, believing America would not retaliate because of past performance, murdered almost three thousand Americans as the nation watched in stunned disbelief on national television.[7] Two commercial airliners crashed into the twin towers of the World Trade Center; smoke and flames leaped upward. Shocking scenes of Americans leaping to their death are now etched into the brains of millions of Americans.

As brave policemen and New York City firemen dashed into the buildings to rescue their fellow citizens, the buildings collapsed, sending thick clouds of smoke, dust, and debris for blocks in every direction. In a matter of seconds, the dreams and hopes of thousands of families ended in unspeakable horror. It was America's new Day of Infamy.[8]

A third flight, United Airlines Flight 93, was hijacked and crashed in Pennsylvania, where American passengers charged the terrorists bare-handed under the mantra, "Let's roll!" That plane was destined for the White House.[9] God bless the sacred memory of those brave Americans who gave their lives to protect our president.

A fourth flight, American Airlines Flight 77, was hijacked and crashed into the Pentagon. Within minutes, America's symbols of power and pride were in smoldering ruins. More than three thousand people were killed in all four crashes. It was the worst attack on American soil since the British burned the White House in 1813.[10]

It was an act of war! Ladies and gentlemen of America, we are at war with Islamofascism. Jihad has come to America. We are in a war for our survival.

England is at war with radical Islam.

On July 7, 2005, in London, England, Islamic terrorists exploded bombs on three underground trains and a double-decker bus, killing fifty-two people and injuring more than seven hundred.[11]

In 2006, British police arrested twenty-four Islamic terrorists who planned to blow up ten passenger planes flying between Britain and America. Those planes were filled with Americans. It was to be a mass murder of monumental proportions. This was clearly an act of war.

As more details emerged about this thwarted terror plot in London, the *New York Post* reported that two of the suspects in police custody planned to sacrifice their six-month-old son in the name of jihad. Apparently Abdullah Ahmed Ali, age twenty-five, and his wife, Cossor, age twenty-three, secretly plotted to use their child's baby bottle as a liquid bomb to destroy themselves and their child, along with the entire plane.[12]

As horrifying as this is, it is not an isolated phenomenon. In fact, British security experts believe this was only the latest example in the disturbing trend that is growing in popularity among the Islamofascists—a woman using her innocent appearance to dispel suspicions and carry out deadly terrorist attacks.

Even worse is the willingness of many Muslim women to exploit their young children in order to realize their hideous goals. As a security advisor to the British government told *The Sun*, "It may be beyond belief, but we are convinced that there are now women in Britain who are prepared to die with their babies for their twisted cause. They are ruthless, single-minded and totally committed."[13]

France is at war with radical Islam.

A few years ago the world watched on international television as Islamic youth set Paris on fire night after night. It became obvious to the world that these Islamic youths did not move to France to become French; they intended to make France submit to the goals of Islam.

Ten to 12 percent of France is Islamic.[14] A personal friend who returned to America after living in France for five years said that they were awakened one night as Islamic youths marched down the streets in columns, chanting, "Death to the Jews."

Canada is at war with Islamofascists.

In 2006, Islamic terrorists were arrested in Canada with three times the explosives used in the terrorist attack on the Alfred E. Murray Federal Building in Oklahoma City, Oklahoma.[15] What was the objective of these Islamic terrorists in Canada? To capture Canada's prime minister and cut his head off. This is an act of war.

Spain is at war with radical Islam.

Bombs exploded on three commuter trains in Madrid, Spain, on March 11, 2004, killing 201 and injuring 1,400 people. Islamic leaders told Spain to take their troops out of Iraq, and Spain bowed immediately to the demands of radical Islam.[16] Spain is finished as a democracy. Islam has learned that the Spanish government will bow and submit if the terror is sufficient.

Russia and China are at war with America and Israel.

Russia and China have formed an axis power with Iran. China has a multibillion-dollar energy agreement with Iran.[17]

Russia has been helping Iran develop its missile systems and nuclear centers for years. Several years ago former Prime Minister Benjamin Netanyahu of Israel sat in my office and told me that the Mossad, the Israeli intelligence agency, had given him pictorial proof that Russian scientists were helping Iran in the development of their missile systems. That pictorial proof was given to American intelligence before they would believe that Russians were in Iran helping in the development of these nuclear centers.

Russia and China have done everything within their power to protect Iran from sanctions in the United Nations' proceedings. It is very clear that Russia and China have sided with Iran against the United States and Israel.

North Korea is at war with America and Israel.

The world was made acutely aware of North Korea's agenda to push itself into a more prominent nuclear power in recent news. Despite warnings from the United Nations against it, North Korea proceeded with a test of its nuclear missiles on October 8, 2006. The news agency in South Korea says North Korea's test was "aimed at getting the U.S. to the negotiating table" and that North Korea is willing to give up its nuclear weapons and reenter international peace talks only once "the U.S. takes corresponding measures."[18] Clearly, North Korea has an agenda against America. The country is also on the side of the Islamofascists desiring to end America and Israel, since it supplies weapons technology for Iran and Syria.

In considering the parade of nations at war, throw in the Islamic attacks in Pakistan, Afghanistan, Yemen, Kuwait, the Philippines, Egypt, Turkey, Bangladesh, and Thailand.

When you consider all of the nations that are at war for or against Islamofascism, there is no way to escape the logical conclusion that the stage is set for Earth's final moments.

CHAPTER 3

ENTER: THE KING
OF THE NORTH

IT WOULD BE sure fanaticism to suggest that the Bible mentions the word *Russia* in the text. Yet God, through Ezekiel, has made some very clear and specific revelations in the Bible concerning the rise of a great power to the north of Israel that will destroy the peace and stability of the world at the end of days.

Daniel 9:27 informs us that there will rise on the world's scene a man of supernatural power who, Daniel says, "shall destroy many in their prosperity" (Dan. 8:25). This man will come out of the European Union and will try to resolve the Islamic/Israeli dispute now raging in Israel.

This political orator and charismatic personality will make a covenant with Israel for seven years, guaranteeing them safety and protection as a nation. In Scripture he is called the Antichrist, "the son of perdition," meaning Satan's chief son (2 Thess. 2:3). When the events of Ezekiel 38 open, the nation of Israel has been given a covenant by this political leader, who is the head of the European Union.

The Jewish people are confident that the European powers will protect them from any outside aggressor or invader. Israel is aware that Russia is its enemy. For years Israel has known that Russia has been helping Iran develop nuclear weapons to be used against them. This seven-year peace accord between the head of the European Union and Israel is in the near future.

It is important for the reader to understand that Bible prophecy divides world military powers into four sectors just before the end of the age. (See Daniel 2:31–35.) The four great world military powers just before the end of the age are simply called the king of the North, the king of the South, the king of the East, and the king of the West. It is important to remember that all directions in Scripture are given based on their geographic relationship to Israel.

In this chapter I will go into great detail to demonstrate to you that the king of the North is Russia, the king of the South represents the Arab nations, the king of the East is China, and the king of the West is Europe and America.

THE KING OF THE NORTH: RUSSIA

Let us first consider *the king of the North* because it is a kingdom that lies north of Israel.

> And the word of the Lord came unto me, saying, Son of man, set thy face against Gog, the land of Magog, the chief prince of Meshech and Tubal, and prophesy against him.
>
> —EZEKIEL 38:1–2, KJV

Gog is a word for "ruler," which literally means "the man on top." I can't think of a better name for a dictator than Gog.

The verse tells us that Gog was "chief prince" of the land of Magog. *Chief*, which means "head," is the Hebrew word *Rosh*.[1] In his ancient Hebrew lexicon, Wilhelm Gesenius (1786–1842), the great Hebrew scholar, identified *Rosh* as an ancient name for Russia.[2]

In his book *The Destiny of Nations*, Dr. John Cumming said: "The King of the North I conceive to be the autocrat of Russia...that Russia occupies a place and a very momentous place, and the prophetic word has been admitted by almost all expositors."[3]

Ezekiel puts extreme emphasis on the fact that Israel's great enemy would come from the "uttermost north." It is mentioned in Ezekiel 38:6 and 15, and again in Ezekiel 39:2. The King James Version doesn't translate this as accurately as do the Revised Standard Version and the Amplified Bible. The Hebrew word that qualifies north means either "uttermost" or "extreme north." Any map will instantly verify that the extreme north from Israel is Russia.

In 1968, General Moshe Dayan said, "The next great war will not be with the Arabs, but with the Russians."[4] Now we come to the theological phenomenon that helps us to further identify Gog and Magog with Russia.

> And say, Thus saith the Lord GOD; Behold, I am against thee, O Gog, the chief prince of Meshech and Tubal.
>
> —EZEKIEL 38:3, KJV

Throughout the history of Israel, God has said that He is against certain nations that oppress the Jewish people. God destroyed Egypt for their persecution of the Jews. God set His face against Babylon for their destruction of Jerusalem. Now comes a nation in the last days out of the extreme north that will attack Israel, and God says, "I am against thee." It is intriguing to note that Ezekiel is prophesying about a nation that hasn't come into existence. God says He is *against it* because that nation would be an atheistic nation. No other nation has assumed the dominant position of atheism.

All the nations prior to Russia that God opposed were polytheistic. They believed in many gods. At the beginning of time, God did not give a specific commandment against atheism. Yet His first two commandments were against polytheism. "You shall have no other gods before Me" (Exod. 20:3); and, "You shall not make for yourself a carved image, or any likeness of anything that is in heaven above, or that is in the earth beneath, or that is in the water under the earth" (v. 4).

These strong commandments against many gods addressed the problem of polytheism but not of atheism. Through the pen of King David, God covers the topic of atheism in one verse: "The fool has said in his heart, 'There is no God'" (Ps. 14:1). How utterly ridiculous atheism is!

Yet here is a nation that will appear at the end of days, that is in the extreme north, and that will be atheistic. There is no doubt about the fact of Russia's atheistic government under Communism. Joseph Stalin said, "We have deposed the czars of the earth, and we shall now dethrone the Lord of heaven."[5]

When Russia put a rocket, called the *Sputnik*, past the moon, as it neared the sun the following comment was heard on the radio in Russia: "Our rocket has bypassed the moon. It is nearing the sun. We have not discovered God. We have turned out lights in heaven that no man will be able to put on again. We are breaking the yoke of the gospel, the opiate of the masses. Let us go forth, and Christ shall be relegated to mythology."[6]

WHO ARE MESHECH AND TUBAL?

God declares He is against Gog, the chief prince of Meshech and Tubal. Who is this chief prince? In order to identify these names, we must turn to Genesis 10 where we read about the generations of the sons of Noah: Shem, Ham, and Japheth (v. 1).

In verse 2, the sons of Japheth are given as: "Gomer, Magog, Madai, Javan, Tubal, Meshech, and Tiras." All of the names referred to in Ezekiel 38 are the sons of Japheth.

Ethnologists—historians who track the migrations of people—tell us that after Noah's flood, the Japhethites migrated from Asia Minor to the north, beyond the Caspian and Black Seas. They settled in the area of Rosh that we know today as *Russia*. Wilhelm Gesenius, a world-class Hebrew scholar of the early nineteenth century, discusses the word *Meshech* in his Hebrew lexicon. Gesenius states that the Greek name *Moschi,* derived from the Hebrew name *Meschech*, is the source of the city of Moscow.[7]

RUSSIA'S INVASION OF ISRAEL

> I will turn you around, put hooks into your jaws, and lead you out, with all your army, horses, and horsemen, all splendidly clothed, a great company with bucklers and shields, all of them handling swords.
>
> —EZEKIEL 38:4

Why will Russia come to Israel? Let's take a look at some of the reasons for Russia's interest in dominating Israel.

1. Russia will come to Israel because they need a warm-water entrance into the oceans of the world. The Middle East offers that. Russia, under Putin's leadership, made a $50 billion oil contract with Saddam Hussein and has allowed Russian scientists to direct Iran's nuclear weapons programs to destroy Israel. Putin is the former director of the KGB who has removed

the democratic process from Russia and, at the same time, charmed the West into neutrality.

2. Russia needs oil to regain its military superpower status. Russia hungers for Arabian oil. They must have it to regain their global status, which they lost in the crash of the former Soviet Union.

3. The mineral deposits in the Dead Sea are so great they can't be properly appraised on today's market. It is estimated that the Dead Sea contains two billion tons of potassium chloride, which is potash needed to enrich the soil that is rapidly being depleted around the world. The Dead Sea also contains twenty-two billion tons of magnesium chloride and twelve billion tons of sodium chloride. The wealth of the Dead Sea has the Russian bear salivating at the mouth.

Through Ezekiel, God said to Russia: "I will put hooks in your jaws." God is going to drag Russia into Israel. Why? Throughout its history, Russia has been anti-Semitic and, in its final form, will be led by a dictator who will lead an Arab coalition of nations to crush Israel. God makes it clear that He will judge Russia in the land of Israel, and Russia will not come out alive.

Chapter 4

RUSSIA'S SUPPORTING CAST

W HO ARE THE allies of Russia who will join them in this unholy war to destroy the nation of Israel and exterminate the Jews? God gives their names and addresses through the prophet Ezekiel.

> Persia, Ethiopia, and Libya are with them, all of them with shield and helmet; Gomer and all its troops; the house of Togarmah from the far north and all its troops—many people are with you.
> —EZEKIEL 38:5–6

Persia

Persia is modern-day Iran. In recent years, Russia and Iran have joined forces to create long-range nuclear missiles that can hit London, Jerusalem, and New York. During the administration of former Prime Minister

Benjamin Netanyahu, Israeli intelligence gave photographic proof that Russian scientists were directing and supervising Iran's nuclear weapons programs.

There is no doubt a nuclear collision is coming in the near future in the Middle East. If Israel bombs Iran's eight nuclear sites with laser-guided, bunker-buster bombs, it could easily launch Ezekiel's war, described in Ezekiel 38–39.

Ethiopia and Libya

Ethiopia and Libya are used in two distinctly different senses in the Old Testament. There were nations in Africa known as Ethiopia and Libya, and their names continue until today. There were also states adjacent to Persia that were known as Ethiopia and Libya. When Moses fled from Egypt because he had killed the Egyptian, he went into the wilderness, and there he married an Ethiopian. He did not go south into African Ethiopia but went into the Ethiopia of the Arabian Peninsula, where he married an Ethiopian who was a Shemite. Therefore when Ezekiel speaks of Persia, Ethiopia, and Libya, he is speaking of the Arab states.

When Ezekiel writes concerning Russia in chapter 38, verse 6, he says that: "many people are with you." He repeats that concept in verse 9: "You [Russia] will ascend, coming like a storm, covering the land like a cloud, you and all your troops and many peoples with you." I believe this is a clear suggestion that America's influence with Arab nations will become virtually nonexistent. However, Russia's influence will dramatically increase as they join forces against Israel at the end of this age.

We are watching this courtship between Russia and Iran in daily media reports right now. Shortly after the election of Iran's president, a Russian government spokeswoman stated:

> "The heads of SCO member states congratulated Ahmadinejad on his re-election" in the 2009 Iranian presidential election. Russian Deputy Foreign Minister Sergei Ryabkov characterized the Iranian elections as an "internal affair" and stated that "we welcome the fact that elections took place, we welcome the...[Iranian] president on Russian soil and see it as symbolic that he made his first visit to Russia. This allows hope for progress in bilateral relations."[1]

In further indication of the growing relationship between Russia and Iran, Russia has also warned the United States against taking any military action against Iran or its nuclear facilities and has criticized the United States for imposing sanctions against a Russian state-owned defense contractor that had reportedly sold dual-use military technology to Iran.[2]

What does the evolving relationship between Iran and Russia mean for the surrounding Arab nations? They believe the Islamic fanatical vision of exterminating the Jews can be realized with Russia's help. Absolute control of Jerusalem as the capital for the new Palestinian state will be within their grasp.

However, there is one problem looming on the horizon: God Almighty, whom the Russians defy and Islamics denounce, has brought this evil axis of power into Israel to bury it before the eyes of the world. The destruction of Russia and its Islamic allies is going to be the most powerful object lesson the world has seen since Pharaoh and his army were drowned in the Red Sea.

Ezekiel writes to the Russian leadership of this Russian-Arab coalition of nations, saying:

> Prepare yourself and be ready, you and all your companies that are gathered about you; and be a guard for them.
>
> —EZEKIEL 38:7

A better translation of the phrase "be a guard for them" is this: "Be thou a commander unto them." Ezekiel leaves no doubt that Russia is leading the attack.

In verse 8, Russia makes its move into Israel. "After many days you will be visited. In the latter years [at the end of the age] you will come into the land [Israel] of those brought back from the sword."

Verse 11 reveals the fact that Israel has made a covenant with the false messiah out of the European Union who promises peace and safety. But the Bible warns, "For when they say, 'Peace and safety!' then sudden destruction comes upon them" (1 Thess. 5:3).

In Ezekiel 38:11, Russia is addressing all its allies, suggesting they go into Israel, which is called the "land of unwalled villages." Russia says, "I will go to them that are at rest, that dwell safely." Why is Israel at rest? It is at rest because its leaders are trusting in their peace accord with the European Union to guarantee their safety from Russia and the Arab coalition of nations.

Since the collapse of the Soviet Union and the end of the Cold War, relations between Russia and Israel have been on the upswing. A fact sheet on Russia-Israel relations, posted on the Internet on July 30, 2010, states:

> Israel is home to the world's largest diaspora of Russian speakers outside of non-Russian-speaking countries. The two nations have a growing trade relationship, and a business venture involving Russian and Israeli scientists has

produced and successfully tested a fuel tank for hydrogen-powered cars. Meanwhile, security cooperation continues as both countries face the threat of terrorism from radical Islamist groups. Next year, Russia and Israel will celebrate 20 years of continuous diplomatic relations. Russia takes over the rotating presidency of the UN Security Council Aug. 1.[3]

Ezekiel 38:11 suggests that a day is coming in the future when Russia will "go to them that are at rest." Watch for Russian-Israeli relations to become politically sensitive in days to come.

AMERICA AND THE MIDDLE EAST CONFLICT

Now let's look at the coming crisis with Iran. Iran is rapidly developing nuclear weapons to use against Israel and America and is ready to share its nuclear technology with other Islamic nations. The president of Iran, Mahmoud Ahmadinejad, has said on international television, "With respect to the needs of Islamic countries, we are ready to transfer nuclear know-how to these countries."[4] That means every Islamic terrorist organization is going to have the opportunity to use these atomic weapons. Now think about that. That means suitcase bombs could be exploding in several of the major cities of America at the same time. Imagine the chaos and confusion of a dozen Katrinas happening at the same time, created by the devastation of atomic suitcase bombs. Each bomb could kill up to a million people if exploded in a highly populated area like New York City. You say it can't happen. You're exactly wrong. Eugene Habiger, former Executive Chief of Strategic Weapons at the Pentagon, said that an event of nuclear mega-terrorism on US soil is "not a matter of if but when."[5]

In the 2011 meeting of the World Economic Forum in Davos, Switzerland, Yukiya Amano, director general of the International Atomic Energy Agency (IAEA), made this statement:

> Another risk is nuclear material falling into the hands of terrorists. Some people do not believe this is a real risk. But the IAEA has a database and, on average, every two days we receive information about the illicit trafficking of nuclear materials or radioactive materials and this may only be the tip of the iceberg.[6]

Amano told Fox News, "Nowadays, with the current level of world technology, terrorists can make nuclear weapons—well, dirty bombs, at least."[7]

When forty-seven world leaders met in Washington DC in early 2010, the focus of the two-day conference was to discuss ways of securing loose nuclear material around the world. This delegation of world leaders was the largest to meet in sixty years.[8]

When the CIA confiscated records from the computer of Dr. Sultan Bashiruddin Mahmood, former chairman of Pakistan's Atomic Energy Commission, at his bogus charity in Kabul, they discovered evidence that at least one al Qaeda nuke had been forward deployed to the United States from Karachi in a cargo container. On October 11, 2001, George Tenet, former CIA director, met with President Bush to inform him that at least two tactical nukes had reached al Qaeda operatives in the United States. This news was substantiated by Pakistan's ISI, the CIA, and the FBI.[9]

In addition, Paul L. Williams, a former consultant to the FBI on terrorism, indicates that there is empirical proof that al Qaeda possesses nukes. British agents posing as recruits infiltrated al Qaeda training camps in Afghanistan in 2000. In another instance, an al Qaeda operative was arrested at Ramallah with a tactical nuke strapped to his back. And US military officials discovered a lead canister containing uranium-238 in Kandahar at the outset of Operation Enduring Freedom.[10]

If you are having trouble believing that teams of terrorists maintaining a nuclear weapon in the United States wouldn't be detected, think about this. Williams reports that there isn't just one team, but at least seven.[11] They are working within mosques and Islamic centers. In the United States, a federal judge will not provide any FBI or law enforcement agent with a warrant to search a mosque of an Islamic center for any reason since such places are listed as "houses of worship."[12]

The seven areas that have been identified are New York, Miami, Houston, Las Vegas, Los Angeles, Chicago, and Washington DC. The attacks will occur simultaneously at the seven sites.

Early in 2011, the spiritual leader of Iran, Ayatollah Ali Khamenei, warned the United States to stay out of his country's business, and, in particular, its nuclear program. Speaking on a tour of southeast Iran, Khamenei said the United States "deserved a punch in the mouth."[13]

In an article titled, "Electronics to Determine Fate of Future Wars," an Iranian military journal explains how an EMP attack on America's electronic infrastructure, caused by the detonation of a nuclear weapon high above the United States, would bring the country to its knees.

"Once you confuse the enemy communication network you can also disrupt the work of the enemy command- and decision-making center," the article states. "Even worse today when you disable a country's military high command through disruption of communications, you will, in effect, disrupt all the affairs of that country. If the world's industrial countries fail to devise effective ways to defend themselves against dangerous electronic assaults then they will disintegrate within a few years. American soldiers would not be able to find food to eat nor would they be able to fire a single shot."[14]

The journal publicly floated the idea of launching an electromagnetic pulse attack as the key to defeating the United States.

Listen up—this is extremely important.

Here's what the EMP does. This electromagnetic blanket does not kill people—it kills electrons. In short, it stops every form of electricity instantly and for months, maybe years.[15] Here's how it could be used against America in warfare.

A fake satellite crossing over America at the height of 280 miles suddenly explodes over the Great Plains of the United States, releasing several pounds of enriched plutonium, blanketing the United States of America with gamma rays. Instantly, in one-billionth of a second, all electrical power is cut off, and cut off for months.

No lights or refrigeration will work in your home. Every ounce of food you have will rot in your freezer. Your car won't work because it starts with electricity. Trucks won't work, meaning transportation bringing you everything you use will stop. All machinery will stop. The radio and the television stations will go off the air. Planes that are in flight will crash because their electronic systems will fail. The missile systems will fail to function. We will cease to be a superpower in one-billionth of a second.

The president will not be able to communicate with his military people in the field because the phones will not work. America's refineries will shut down. There will be no gas and no oil. The gas at the service station won't be available because those pumps get the gas out of the ground with electricity. Computers won't work, which means city, state, and government offices will be shut down. There will be a nationwide food and gas shortage within a few days.

You say that can't happen? There are people who are planning it right now. It's not new. It's been talked about for twenty years. Only now, rogue states have the ability to put this weapon to use, and it will happen unless Iran and the "axis of evil" are stopped![16]

Can Iran do it? Our government says yes. North Korea, an ally of Iran, also has that ability. Iran is presently ruled by Islamic fanatics who would be more than willing to use those weapons against America and Israel. North Korea is ruled by an absolute madman who is reported to be schizophrenic and paranoid.

The *Congressional Report* reads: "Even primitive Scud missiles could be used for this purpose [electronic blankets]. And top U.S. intelligence officials reminded members of Congress that there is a glut of these missiles on the world market. They are currently being bought and sold for about $100,000 apiece."[17]

Now think about that!

This great, magnificent nation that is so technically oriented has created an Achilles' heel—electricity. With one $100,000 missile fired from a used submarine two hundred miles offshore and a few pounds of enriched plutonium exploding over the United States, every form of electricity would stop instantly and for months. In one second we would be living in the nineteenth century.

Where is the world headed?

What is in the immediate future?

If Iran is not stopped in its quest for nuclear weapons,

the Iranians will have them soon—and they will use them against Israel. If Iran is stopped, it will happen through military force. Only America and Israel have that power, because Russia is now helping Iran to develop their nuclear weapons. I believe this military action will lead to Russia bringing together a coalition of Islamic nations to invade Israel. The prophet Ezekiel paints that portrait clearly in Ezekiel chapters 38 and 39. We will take a closer look at Ezekiel's picture of what is to come in the Middle East in this book.

CHINA: THE KING OF THE EAST

The Bible warns us of the coming rising importance of this king of the East. Revelation 16:12 (NAS) records:

> The sixth angel poured out his bowl upon the great river, the Euphrates; and its water was dried up, so that the way would be prepared for the kings from the east.

John the Revelator described an incredible marching army of two hundred million soldiers from the Orient, marching down the dried-up riverbed of the Euphrates toward Israel. Why would China make this move? China is also thirsty for Arab oil.

When the United States went to war with Iraq in

2003, China began to make a huge shift in its oil policies. Until then, most of China's oil had come from Iraq. But with the entry of America into the country of Iraq, China could no longer put all its "oil apples" in the one basket of Iraq's oil reserves. "Iraq changed the government's thinking," said Pan Rui, an international relations expert at Fudan University in Shanghai.[18]

The two kings that remain on the earth at this point in prophecy are the king of the West, which is being led by the Antichrist, and the king of the East, which is China. These two kings and their armies will meet to battle it out for world supremacy on a battlefield in Israel called *Armageddon*.

CHAPTER 5

AMERICA—TOO LATE, TOO LITTLE?

W HERE IS AMERICA in this picture? In Ezekiel 38:12, Russia and its allies are going into Israel "to take plunder and to take booty." Russia is going to move militarily against Israel from the north to seize the great mineral wealth and natural resources that are there. They will promise the Islamic nations control of Jerusalem and the Temple Mount. What will be America's response to this brazen act of invading and raping Israel of its wealth? Ezekiel answers in verse 13.

"Sheba, Dedan, the merchants of Tarshish" (that is, the Western powers) will be upset when Russia invades Israel. These nations "and all their young lions" (England's symbol is that of a lion, and America is an offspring of England; hence, the "young lions") will not come to

Israel's rescue. They will not send massive military forces to drive Russia and the Arabs out of Israel. Instead, the Western world is simply going to make a passive diplomatic response, saying:

> Have you gathered your army to take booty, to carry away silver and gold, to take away livestock and goods, to take great plunder?
>
> —EZEKIEL 38:13

What a ridiculous response!

It's obvious to the nations of the world what Russia and the Arabs are doing, and yet the Western world is doing absolutely nothing to stop them. Why won't America respond? Our current democratic administration has already given the order for our military to withdraw from Iraq and has said that America would reach out to other countries as "an equal partner" rather than as the "exceptional" nation that many before him had embraced. "Our problems must be dealt with through partnership" and "progress must be shared," has been his approach to Middle East issues.[1]

But the troubles sweeping the Middle East—including the recent crisis in Egypt, which is still taking place as this book is being written—are making it clear that it is time to find a new strategy that treats the Middle East as more than a distraction. In a recent article James Carafano states:

> The White House needs to set clear and unequivocal expectations for how the government in Cairo should treat its own people. Next, the Administration must make clear it will finish the job in Iraq and keep the U.S. forces and resources in place that the government in Baghdad needs to complete its transition to a secure and sovereign state that can protect itself and look after the needs of its own citizens. Obama must also revitalize the partnership with Israel. Israel remains America's most important and reliable ally in the region. And the White House must go after the regime in Iran. Sanctions and political isolation have hurt Iran, but the administration has been reluctant to press for further sanctions or ensure the full implementation of the ones on the books. That is a huge mistake. The most effective means to tame the regime in Tehran and help lay the foundation for its eventual demise is to stiffen U.S. resolve to isolate and punish the regime for fostering terrorism, promoting an Islamist agenda, pursuing nuclear weapons, and causing suffering and loss of liberty to the Iranian people.[2]

America as a whole wants short, high-tech military campaigns with shock and awe that end in Washington DC with massive parades down Pennsylvania Avenue on national television, such as we had in Desert Storm. Long, drawn-out wars of attrition, as in Vietnam, will be part of our past—not our future. When America sees Russia and the Arabs going into Israel, it will be simply a war above and beyond its national will to respond. Russia and the Arab nations will form one of the most impressive military forces ever put together. As Ezekiel says, "It will cover the land."

Ezekiel makes it clear that America's and Europe's diplomatic inquiry means absolutely nothing to Russia and the Arabs. The invasion is on! This invasion is described as follows:

> You will come up against My people Israel like a cloud, to cover the land. It will be in the latter days that *I will bring you against My land*, so that the nations may know Me, when I am hallowed in you, O Gog, before their eyes.
>
> —EZEKIEL 38:16, EMPHASIS ADDED

God makes it clear that He is dragging Russia and its allies into Israel: "I will bring you against My land."

When Russia leads its Arab allies into Israel, the Western superpowers simply watch.

I believe that after years of repeated acts of violent terrorism by Islamic fanatics—such as Madrid, Spain; September 11, 2001, in New York City; and the brutal attack in the London subways of July 7, 2005, killing about fifty people and wounding hundreds—the Western nations have become gun-shy about attacking a Russian-Arab military force.

Whatever the reason, Ezekiel portrays Russia as being in complete command. Why? Because the defender of Israel, the God of Abraham, Isaac, and Jacob, has a hook in Russia's jaw, dragging it into Israel for the greatest object lesson the world has ever seen.

There is comfort and consolation in Ezekiel's prophetic portrait of the world tomorrow. The message is that God is in total control of what appears to be a hopeless situation for Israel. He has dragged these anti-Semitic nations to the nations of Israel to crush them so that the Jews of Israel as a whole will confess that He is the Lord. America and Europe will not save Israel—God will!

Ezekiel reveals a day coming when God's fury explodes against the nations that have tormented His chosen people for so long. Ezekiel writes God's description of His anger: "My fury will show in My face" (Ezek. 38:18).

The Weapons of War

God will destroy Russia and its Arab allies with three weapons of war that He has used before in Scripture. These weapons are:

1. A mighty earthquake

2. Every man's sword against his brother

3. Raining from heaven of fire and brimstone

One day soon there will a battle scene report on the evening news via global television that will reach the nations of the world with these words:

> "In My jealousy and in the fire of My wrath I have spoken: 'Surely in that day there shall be a great earthquake in the land of Israel, so that the fish of the sea, the birds of the heavens, the beasts of the fields, all creeping things that creep on the earth, and all men who are on the face of the earth shall shake at My presence. The mountains shall be thrown down, the steep places shall fall, and every wall shall fall to the ground.' I will call for a sword against Gog [Russia] throughout all My mountains," says the Lord GOD. "Every man's sword will be against his brother. And I will bring him

to judgment with pestilence and bloodshed; I will rain down on him, on his troops, and on the many peoples who are with him [Arab nations], flooding rain, great hailstones, fire, and brimstone."

—EZEKIEL 38:19–22

When did God use these weapons of war before?

When Moses's leadership was being contested by Korah, Dathan, and Abiram in Numbers 16, God told Moses to get away from their tents because He was about to give Israel an object lesson never to be forgotten in the history of the world.

Moses records the scene:

"But if the Lord creates a new thing, and the earth opens its mouth and swallows them up with all that belongs to them, and they [those who were rejecting Moses's leadership] go down alive into the pit, then you will understand that these men have rejected the Lord." Now it came to pass, as he finished speaking all these words, that the ground split apart under them, and the earth opened its mouth and swallowed them up, with their households and all the men with Korah, with all their goods.

—NUMBERS 16:30–32

The world is heading toward God's second object lesson. Ezekiel makes it clear that God will send an earthquake that will swallow up the enemies of Israel, just as an earthquake swallowed up the enemies of Moses.

God will use the sword of brother against brother as the second weapon of war. When God sent Gideon to destroy the Midianites, Gideon commanded his meager fighting force of three hundred men to sound the trumpets and to break the pitchers. The Midianites turned their swords against each other in massive confusion and slaughtered one another. (See Judges 7.)

God will bring this battle-tested tactic to wage war against Russia and its allies when they come against Israel. God will cause confusion to come among them as they turn and fight each other, slaughtering each other in history's greatest demonstration of friendly fire.

The third weapon in God's arsenal is great hailstones, fire, and brimstone. Two of the most infamous cities that ever existed in history were the cities of Sodom and Gomorrah. Why are they famous? Their fame arises from the fact that they no longer exist. These are the two cities where God poured out fire and brimstone because of their great sin and iniquity, and they were obliterated from the earth.

To this day geologists have sought to discover the

location of Sodom and Gomorrah, but God so completely destroyed them they have never been found. Some speculate that they have been buried beneath the Dead Sea, which would explain the rare sulfuric odor and the taste of the water in the Dead Sea.

When Russia and its allies invade Israel, and America and Europe fail to respond, "He who sits in the heavens shall laugh" (Ps. 2:4) as He crushes the Russian-Arab tormenters of the apple of His eye. He will crush them as he crushed Pharaoh, Haman, and Hitler so that Israel and the world "shall know that I am the LORD" (Ezek. 38:23).

CHAPTER 6

SHOCK AND AWE—
GOD'S REVENGE

PAUL'S LETTER TO the Christians in Rome has the literary framework of a lawyer establishing and presenting the principle pleas in his case carefully and accurately before the Judge of all judges. Paul's epistle to the Romans represents the Alps of theological thought. Romans 9–11 is the breathtaking and mind-stretching pinnacle of God's revelation to man.

Romans 9–11 has long been the acid test in Pauline exegesis. This awesome pinnacle of theological thought forces us to examine the historical advantages of Judaism, free will, and divine election and to ask ourselves: What is God doing with Israel today, and why?

As we enter the twenty-first century, the State of Israel has now been gathered by the mighty right hand of God and flourishes as the only democratic society in the Middle East. How are we to treat the promises of God toward Israel and the Jewish people? Some evangelicals teach that God has replaced Israel. This is an anti-Semitic theology that refuses to believe God still has a place in His heart for Israel and the Jewish people. Something that has been replaced vanishes and is no longer heard of. It becomes extinct, just as Sodom and Gomorrah are eternally buried. How can something that's been replaced be functioning with such dynamic force and vitality? The nation of Israel dominates the news.

In Romans 11:5, Paul speaks of a "remnant." No one can study Paul's writings today without an awareness of the challenge to biblical interpretation that the Holocaust presents. Are the Holocaust survivors mentioned in verse 5 the "remnant," which can be legitimately translated as "survivors"? In verse 26, Paul boldly states, "All Israel will be saved." In verses 25–26 he speaks of a "mystery," one that is never explained.

I am fully aware that very few pastors or Bible teachers preach or teach from this theological minefield. Why? Because the complexity of Romans 9–11 is difficult, and the verses pull us in directions we find uncomfortable. When we are compelled by a preponderance of truth to accept a position our denomination rejects, it's easier to *ignore* Scripture than to *interpret* Scripture. Paul's teachings in Romans 9–11 will stretch your mind—and mind stretching, like any other kind of rigorous exercise, can be painful.

Diamonds are not found in the dust; they're buried deep in the breast of the earth, and their discovery brings great reward. Paul told Timothy, "All Scripture is given by inspiration of God" (2 Tim. 3:16). No Christian is any stronger than his or her knowledge of the Word of God. Now, let's start digging for diamonds together!

Let's begin at the beginning!

Initially, let's understand this is not intended to be an exhaustive, theological treatise on these titanic chapters. Such a discourse would require several hundred pages to cover adequately.

There are ten basic thoughts I would like to plant in the fertile soil of your mind for your prayerful consideration. Before you throw this book away in the fire, read this whole section, because the puzzle will come together. The ten concepts are as follows:

1. *Romans 9–11 is a magnificent codicil, which is a stand-alone document.* When a lawyer makes a will, then remembers there is something he wishes to add to the will

after it has been written, the portion added is called a *codicil*. The codicil modifies the original document and becomes part of the whole. Romans 9–11 is a divine codicil by Saint Paul concerning God's post-Calvary position on the Jewish people.

2. *There are eight biblical evidences that this stand-alone document, this codicil, could not refer to anyone but the Jewish people.*

3. *Who is a Jew?* This is a very controversial matter to this very day in Israel and around the world.

4. *There is the enormously controversial doctrine of election, that God chooses to save some and allow others to be lost.* I will present why I believe this doctrine applies exclusively to the Jewish people and does not apply to Gentile believers. I repeat: Do not throw the book in the fire just yet.

5. *Has God rejected Israel?* We will explore this concept.

6. *Are all Jews eternally lost?* Not one Christian in ten thousand can correctly answer this question.

7. *Why did God judicially blind the Jewish people to the identity of Messiah?* This concept is totally foreign to evangelicals.

8. *As we examine the historical roots of Christianity,* we will discover that they are Jewish!

9. *A glimpse at Israel's future* reveals the "mystery" Paul refused to resolve in Romans chapter 11.

10. Saint Paul boldly declares, *"All Israel will be saved."* This is the final concept we will explore.

Let's return to the first concept, that Romans 9–11 is a theological codicil, which makes it a stand-alone document. A casual reading of Romans reveals the obvious fact that Romans chapters 1 through 8 represent one common theme—justification and sanctification. Every chapter is connected and flows with this specific theme.

As you continue reading, it is instantly obvious that

chapters 9, 10, and 11 have nothing to do whatsoever with chapters 1 through 8 or 12 through 16.

Chapters 9 through 11 are completely unique in their theme, which is the Jewish people. These chapters are a legal insert separating chapters 1 through 8 from chapters 12 through 16. The fact is that Romans 9–11 is a stand-alone document and represents God's post-Calvary position paper on the Jewish people. Proving this point even further is the fact that Romans 12–16 could easily follow Romans 1–8 in thought and structure without breaking the flow of Paul's thesis.

After accepting Romans 9–11 as a stand-alone document, I, therefore, choose to interpret this theological document respecting the primary principles of *hermeneutics*, which is the science of interpreting Scripture. To do so we must address these things:

1. Who wrote this document?

2. To whom was it written?

3. For what purpose was the document written?

4. All scripture is to be interpreted by other scripture to avoid human error or personal bias.

We are getting ready to take a swim in an extremely swift theological stream. What is presented here cannot be my opinion—it must be the *yea* and *amen* of the sacred Word of God.

The answers to 1, 2, and 3 are as follows: The Book of Romans was written by Saint Paul to the Christians in Rome to explain God's position on the Jewish people (Rom. 11:1, 11) and God's plan of salvation for Israel (v. 26).

GREAT SORROW FOR A GREAT PEOPLE: ROMANS 9:1–4

I tell the truth in Christ, I am not lying, my conscience also bearing me witness in the Holy Spirit, that I have great sorrow and continual grief in my heart. For I could wish that I myself were accursed from Christ for my brethren, my countrymen according to the flesh, who are Israelites, to whom pertain the adoption, the glory, the covenants, the giving of the law, the service of God, and the promises; of whom are the fathers and from whom, according to the flesh, Christ came, who is over all, the eternally blessed God. Amen.

—ROMANS 9:1–4

In chapter 8, Paul carries us to the stars with his emotional oration that nothing can separate a believer from the love of God. Then, as quickly as lightning flashes from east to west, his mood radically changes as he opens chapter 9, saying, "I have great sorrow and unceasing anguish in my heart for the Jewish people."

Remember that the Jews hated Paul. They considered him a traitor to Judaism. Paul tells us, "From the Jews five times I received forty stripes minus one," adding that he was in constant "perils of my own countrymen" (2 Cor. 11:24, 26).

Just as Jesus wept over Jerusalem concerning the coming Roman invasion that would destroy the temple, demolish Jerusalem, and turn the streets red with Jewish blood (Luke 19:41–44), just so Saint Paul felt great sorrow for the Jewish people, to the point of being willing to be placed under God's curse if it would help his brothers, his own people, his own flesh and blood—the people of Israel.

Paul responded as Moses did when Israel built the golden calf while God was giving him the Ten Commandments on top of Mount Sinai. Moses prayed, "These people have committed a great sin, and have made for themselves a god of gold! Yet now, if You will forgive their sin—but if not, I pray, blot me out of Your book which You have written" (Exod. 32:31–32). The "book" Moses spoke about is none other than the Book of Life of Revelation 20:12.

Most Christians do not know that all Torah Jews on High Holy days (Rosh Hashanah and Yom Kippur) attend the synagogue where the liturgy calls for Jews to pray that their sins would be forgiven and their names written in the Book of Life.

PAUL'S EIGHT BIBLICAL EVIDENCES CONCERNING THE JEWISH PEOPLE

There are eight scriptural evidences that indicate that Romans 9–11 refer exclusively to the Jewish people. Let's consider each one briefly:

1. Adoption as sons

The nation of Israel was made God's children, which is clearly confirmed in Exodus 4:22: "Thus says the LORD: '*Israel is My son*, My firstborn'" (emphasis added). The Greek word used in Romans 9:7 for *children* is the same as the one used in Romans 8:16: "The Spirit Himself bears witness with our spirit that we are children of God."

Israel alone received the glory, the covenants, the Law, the directions for tabernacle worship, and the promises. Theirs are the patriarchs and the prophets, and, ultimately, they are the human source of Jesus Christ. Israel alone is referred to by God as "My son."

2. The divine glory

Only the Jewish people experienced the *Shekinah glory*, which means "the glorious presence of God." This was visible in the pillar of fire that led Israel from Egypt to the Promised Land. (See Exodus 13:21; 33:9; Numbers 12:5; 14:14.)

This visible presence of God was present in the tabernacle in the wilderness (Exod. 40:36–38) and in the temple when it was built in Jerusalem (Ezek. 1:28; 3:23; 9:3). The visible presence of God will return to Jerusalem when Messiah rules the earth from the Temple Mount, ushering in the Golden Age of Peace. There shall be no need of moon or stars by night or of sun to shine by day. The manifest presence of God from the presence of Messiah will cause the city of Jerusalem to glow perpetually with Shekinah glory.

3. The covenants are theirs.

The God of the Bible is a covenant God, and He never breaks covenant. Moses tells us:

> Therefore know that the LORD your God, He is God, the faithful God who keeps covenant...for a thousand generations.
>
> —DEUTERONOMY 7:9

The covenants God makes with His people are everlasting, without end, and actually translated "longer than forever." These covenants are not based on man's faithfulness to God; they're based on God's faithfulness to man. Those who teach that God has broken covenant with the Jewish people teach a false doctrine based on scriptural ignorance and a narcissistic attitude.

God made a covenant with Abraham, saying:

> I will make you a great nation;
> I will bless you and make your name great;
> And you will be a blessing.
> I will bless those who bless you,
> And I will curse him who curses you;
> And in you all the families of the earth shall be
>   blessed.
>
> —GENESIS 12:2–3

God made a blood covenant with Abraham, giving him and his descendants the land of Israel (Gen. 15:9–21). That covenant was renewed in Genesis 17:7–14 and again in Genesis 22. The covenant was extended to Isaac and to Jacob at Bethel. (See Genesis 28; Exodus 2:24; 6:3–5.)

God gave a covenant to King David in Psalm 105:8–11 concerning the Jewish right to own and possess the land of Israel forever. Then God gave David a covenant that his "throne would be established forever" (2 Sam. 7:12–13, 16). This was a reference to Jesus Christ, who was introduced in His ministry as "the Son of David." In the future, He shall rule the earth forever from the city of Jerusalem, and "every knee should bow…and that every tongue should confess that Jesus Christ is Lord, to the glory of God the Father" (Phil. 2:10–11).

The concept of covenant is so important in the plan of God for man that it is mentioned 256 times in the Old Testament. Covenant is the soil in which every flower grows in Scripture. God does nothing, not ever, of importance without covenant. Evangelicals who teach that God broke covenant with the Jewish people can have absolutely no confidence that God will not break covenant with the Gentiles.

4. The receiving of the Law

The Law is actually the Torah—the written Word of God. It is a misunderstanding for Christians to call it "the Law of Moses." It is not the Law of Moses; it is the

Law of God as given to Moses on Mount Sinai for all humanity to read, honor, and obey.

When Paul wrote his letter to the Romans, the Torah had been in existence for more than 1,300 years. Think about that! America has existed only 235 years as of 2011.

The giving of the Torah from God to Moses on top of Mount Sinai was where the divine and eternal met the human and temporal. It is important for Christians to remember that Jesus was a rabbi who introduced Himself as the living Torah, "Word of God."

> In the beginning [Genesis 1:1] was the Word [Torah], and the Word was with God, and the Word was God.... And the Word became flesh [Jesus Christ of Nazareth] and dwelt among us, and we beheld His glory, the glory as of the only begotten of the Father, full of grace and truth.
>
> —JOHN 1:1, 14

The Torah was given to the Jewish people thousands of years before the Gentiles knew it existed (Rom. 3:1–2).

5. The temple worship

Temple worship refers to the elaborate set of regulations for construction of the temple as well as the exact sacrificial system that would cleanse Israel from sin.

The symbolism of the temple was a physical portrait of God's plan for man. The temple was surrounded by a fence of white fabric, symbolizing holiness and separation from the world.

The entrance to the temple complex had only one door, as Jesus Christ said of Himself: "I am the door. If anyone enters by Me, he will be saved" (John 10:9). The doors to the temple were very wide, fulfilling the words of Jesus, "Whosoever will come…" (Mark 8:34, KJV).

The first item found inside was the laver for the washing of the hands. It was necessary that a person be purified before that person approached the altar for the forgiveness of sins. The laver was lined with mirrors so you could see yourself as you washed your hands. "Examine yourselves as to whether you are in the faith" (2 Cor. 13:5).

Next was the altar where the sacrifice was presented to God by the priest. It was a daily reminder to all Israel that "without the shedding of blood there is no forgiveness" (Heb. 9:22, NIV).

Then came the temple itself, whose symbolism and process of atonement are worthy of a book all by themselves. If you do not understand God's message to mankind through the symbolism of the tabernacle, you do not understand the Word of God. I have a six-hour teaching on the tabernacle that will give you a glimpse of the glory and boundless majesty of the God of Abraham, Isaac, and Jacob.

It was only to the Jewish people that God gave the temple and its fathomless revelations concerning God's plan for man.

6. The promises

The Old Testament is filled with promises of many kinds, but "the promises" in Romans 9:4 refer to the promises of redemption to be fulfilled by Messiah, who is Jesus Christ. Saint Paul makes this very clear in Galatians 3.

It was Moses who gave us the first extensive prophetic portrait of the coming Messiah. In Deuteronomy 18:18–19, Moses brings to Israel the following promise from God:

> I will raise up for them a Prophet like you from among their brethren, and will put My words in His mouth, and He shall speak to them all that I command Him. And it shall be that whoever will not hear My words, which He speaks in My name, I will require it of Him.

In Acts 3:22–26, the apostle Peter explains how this prophecy of Moses applies to Jesus Christ of Nazareth as Israel's Messiah.

> For Moses truly said to the fathers, "The LORD your God will raise up for you a Prophet like me from your brethren. Him you shall hear in all things, whatever He says to you. And it shall be that every soul who will not hear that Prophet shall be utterly destroyed from among the people." Yes, and all the prophets, from Samuel and those who follow, as many as have spoken, have also foretold these days. You are sons of the prophets, and of the covenant which God made with our fathers, saying to Abraham, "And in your seed all the families of the earth shall be blessed." To you first, God, having raised up His Servant Jesus, sent Him to bless you, in turning away every one of you from your iniquities.

Moses's words established three facts:

God promised to send to Israel a particular Prophet at a later time. The language Moses uses is singular throughout: "a Prophet"…"Him you shall hear"…"whatever He says." These words cannot describe the later prophets in Israel as a whole. They referred to one special prophet.

This prophet would have unique authority! If anyone in Israel refused to hearken to this prophet, God would bring judgment upon that person.

This Prophet would be like Moses in ways that would distinguish Him from all other prophets. A careful comparison of the lives of the two men reveals many distinct parallels between the lives of Moses and Jesus.

Parallels Between Moses and Jesus
1. Both Moses and Jesus were born in a period when Israel was under foreign rule (Exod. 1:8, 11; Luke 2:1–5).
2. Cruel kings decided that both Moses and Jesus should be killed as infants (Exod. 1:15–17; Matt. 2:16).
3. The faith of both Moses's and Jesus's parents saved their lives (Exod. 2:2–4; Matt. 2:13–14).
4. Both Moses and Jesus found protection for a time with the people of Egypt (Exod. 2:10; Matt. 2:14–15).
5. Both Moses and Jesus displayed unusual wisdom and understanding (Acts 7:22; Luke 2:46–47).
6. Both Moses's and Jesus's characters were marked by meekness and humility (Num. 12:3; Matt. 11:28–30).
7. Both Moses and Jesus were completely faithful to God (Num. 12:7; Heb. 3:1–6).
8. Both Moses and Jesus were rejected by Israel for a time (Exod. 32:1; Matt. 27:21–22).
9. Both Moses and Jesus were criticized by their brothers and sisters (Num. 12:1; John 7:5).

10.	Both Moses and Jesus were received by Gentiles after being rejected by Israel (Exod. 2:15, 21; Acts 13:44–48).
11.	Both Moses and Jesus prayed asking forgiveness for God's people (Exod. 32:31–32; Luke 23:34).
12.	Both Moses and Jesus were willing to bear the punishment of God's people (Exod. 32:31–32; 1 Pet. 3:18).
13.	Both Moses and Jesus spoke with God face-to-face (Num. 12:7–8; John 1:18).
14.	Both Moses and Jesus went up into a high mountain to have communion with God, taking some of their closest followers with them (Exod. 24:9–10; Matt. 17:1, 5).
15.	After their mountaintop experiences, both Moses's and Jesus's faces shone with supernatural glory (Exod. 34:34–35; Matt. 17:2).
16.	God spoke audibly from heaven to both Moses and Jesus (Exod. 19:19–20; John 12:23, 28).
17.	Both Moses's and Jesus's places of burial were attended by angels (Jude 9; Matt. 28:5–6).
18.	Both Moses and Jesus appeared alive after their deaths (Matt. 17:3; John 20:19–20).

These are a few of the scriptural comparisons of Moses and Jesus as God's appointed vessels to the nation of Israel. It is evident that God gave promises to the children of Israel and that those promises were kept.

7. The patriarchs are theirs.

The patriarchs are Abraham, Isaac, and Jacob. God used them to found the nation of Israel and to birth the Jewish people, who became the apple of God's eye. (See Deuteronomy 32:10.) The Jews have blessed the nations of the world from Genesis 12 until this day, and they will continue to do so until Messiah comes.

In Romans 11:27–28, Saint Paul makes this stunning statement: "'For this is My covenant with them [the Jewish people], when I shall take away their sins.'...They [the Jewish people] are beloved for the sake of the fathers." In this verse, "the fathers" refers to the patriarchs—Abraham, Isaac, and Jacob.

Why are the Jewish people loved permanently by God? Not just because "God is love" (1 John 4:8). They are loved "for the patriarchs' sake." God made promises to Abraham, Isaac, and Jacob concerning the future of Israel and the Jewish people, and God will keep those promises. "It is impossible for God to lie" (Heb. 6:18).

There is a critical point in Scripture that cannot be missed here. In the second commandment, God takes a definite position: "...visiting the iniquity of the fathers on the children to the third and fourth generations" (Exod. 20:5).

Then in Exodus 20:6, God takes the positive side and

confirms that those who keep His commandments will have His blessing. The precedent is thus established that if disobedience brings judgment, then obedience brings divine blessing. The good deeds of the fathers add to the blessings of their children for three and four generations to come.

God has made promises to Abraham, Isaac, Jacob, and their descendants, and He must keep them to vindicate His own righteousness. Any Christian theology that teaches that God no longer loves the Jewish people or that God will no longer honor His covenant with them is false doctrine—it's simply not true, for it contradicts the teaching of the New Testament.

8. The Jewish people are the human source of Jesus Christ.

I have preached the gospel for forty-eight years as of the writing of this book. When I stand before a congregation other than Cornerstone Church in San Antonio and refer to Jesus Christ as a Jewish rabbi, the audience will invariably gasp as if they believe He was in fact the first president of the Southern Baptist Convention.

While living on Earth, not only was He a Jew, but He was also the Jew of Jews, faithful to the Law of Moses, which, as He said, He came to fulfill, not to destroy. Without the Law of God as given through Moses, there would be no Christ, no Messiah. Jesus was circumcised. He wore the long, falling earlocks of the Hebrews, keeping His hair uncut at the corners. He would touch no flesh of the pig. He would fast on the day of repentance, would eat no leavened bread at Passover time, and would wash His hands before partaking of food while murmuring the prescribed blessing. And He would wear the ritualistic garment adorned with *tzitzit*.

Jesus was a Jew among Jews, yet the Christian gospel has so twisted truth in history that most of its readers identify Jesus with the Gentiles, whatever that may mean. However, neither Greeks nor Romans, Persians nor Syrians, expected a Messiah, and Jesus could neither speak in their alien tongues nor pray in accord with their alien paganisms.

When Jesus spoke, only Hebrews could and would listen. When He sent out His apostles, only Jews were selected. And when He gave up His soul, it was the daughters of Israel who wept for Him. He was crucified at Calvary with a sign on His head that read: "THE KING OF THE JEWS."

It was Jesus, a Jewish rabbi, who said, "Salvation is of the Jews" (John 4:22).

What does that mean?

It simply means this: When you take away the Jewish

contribution to Christianity, there is no Christianity. When you take away the patriarchs, the prophets, every Word of God written by Jewish hands...when you take away Jesus, Mary, and Joseph...when you take away the twelve disciples and the apostle Paul, you have no Christianity.

Christians owe a debt of gratitude to the Jewish people that has never been repaid. It's time to confess our arrogance toward the Jewish people as anti-Semitism. Anti-Semitism is sin, and as sin, it damns the soul.

These eight evidences as recorded by Saint Paul and listed in Romans 9 verify beyond any reasonable doubt that the message of Romans chapters 9, 10, and 11 is intended exclusively for the Jewish people.[*]

---

[*] This chapter is taken from chapter 14, "The Magnificent Codicil," in *Jerusalem Countdown*.

CHAPTER 7

WHY CHRISTIANS SHOULD SUPPORT ISRAEL

A MERICA IS AT the crossroads! Will we believe and obey the Word of God concerning Israel, or will we continue to equivocate and sympathize with Israel's enemies? Our president has vowed to act against terrorists and those who harbor them while pressing Israel not to retaliate against Palestinian terrorists, who are very much a part of the international terrorist network.

God promises to pour out His judgment on any nation that tries to divide up the land of Israel. Listen to the voice of God as it speaks through His prophet Joel.

I will also gather all nations, and…enter into judgment with them there on account of My

> people, My heritage Israel, whom they scattered
> among the nations; they have also *divided up My
> land.* . . . Multitudes, multitudes in the valley of deci-
> sion! For the day of the Lord is near in the valley of
> decision.
>
> —JOEL 3:2, 14, EMPHASIS ADDED

God's Word is very clear! There will be grave consequences for the nation or nations that attempt to divide
up the land of Israel. God's love for Israel is expressed
in the words of Zechariah: "He who touches you [Israel]
touches the apple of His eye" (Zech. 2:8).

God continues expressing His love for Israel, saying, "I
will bless those who bless you, and I will curse him who
curses you" (Gen. 12:3). This is and has been God's foreign
policy toward the Jewish people from Genesis 12 until
this day. Any man or nation that persecutes the Jewish
people or the State of Israel will receive the swift judgment of God. Today, America finds itself bogged down in
an unprovoked, worldwide war with radical Islamic terrorists with no end in sight. America is very vulnerable
to terrorist attacks in the future, whose consequences
could be much more severe than the three thousand lives
lost on 9/11. This is not a time to provoke God and defy
Him to pour out His judgment on our nation for being a
principal force in the division of the land of Israel.

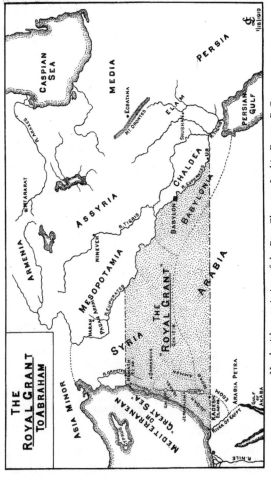

Used with permission of the Rev. Clarence Larkin Estate, P. O. Box 334, Glenside, PA 19038, USA, 215-576-5590

Biblical Reasons

There are biblical reasons why America and all Bible-believing Christians must stand with Israel and their claim to the land.

1. Israel is the only nation created by a sovereign act of God.

Israel belongs to God Himself! As Creator of heaven and earth (Gen. 1:1), God had the right of ownership to give the land to whomever He chose. God gave the title deed for the land of Israel to Abraham, Isaac, Jacob, and their descendants "forever" (Gen. 15:18; 17:2–8). Ishmael, father of Arabs, was excluded from the title deed to the land in Genesis 17:19–21. Therefore, modern-day Palestinians have no biblical mandate to own the land.

The boundaries of the State of Israel are recorded in Scripture. (See Numbers 34:2–15; Joshua 11:16–23; 13:1–22.) The boundaries are further described in Ezekiel 47:13–28 and all of chapter 48.

On the preceding page is a picture of the Royal Land Grant from God Almighty to Abraham, Isaac, Jacob, and their seed forever.[1]

When God established the nations of the world, He began with Israel. Israel is the center of the universe in the mind of God. (See Deuteronomy 32:8–10; Numbers 34:10–15; Joshua 11:16–22.)

2. Christians owe a debt of eternal gratitude to the Jewish people for their contributions, which gave birth to the Christian faith.

Paul recorded in Romans 15:27, "For if the Gentiles have been partakers of their [the Jews] spiritual things, their duty is also to minister to them in material things."

Jesus Christ, a prominent rabbi from Nazareth, said, "Salvation is of the Jews" (John 4:22). Consider what the Jewish people have given to Christianity:

- The sacred Scripture
- The prophets
- The patriarchs
- Mary, Joseph, and Jesus of Nazareth
- The twelve disciples
- The apostles

It is not possible to say, "I am a Christian," and not love the Jewish people. The Bible teaches that love is not what you say, but love is what you do (1 John 3:18). Someone has said:

A bell is not a bell until you ring it,
A song is not a song until you sing it,
Love in your heart is not put there to stay,
Love is not love until you give it away.[2]

3. Jesus never denied His Jewishness.

While some Christians try to deny the connection between Jesus of Nazareth and the Jews of the world, Jesus never denied His Jewishness. He was born Jewish. He was circumcised on the eighth day in keeping with Jewish tradition. He had His Bar Mitzvah on His thirteenth birthday. He kept the Law of Moses. He wore the prayer shawl Moses commanded all Jewish men to wear. He died on the cross with an inscription over His head, "THE KING OF THE JEWS."

Jesus considered the Jewish people His family. Jesus said, "Verily I say unto you, Inasmuch as ye have done it unto one of the least of these my brethren [the Jewish people...Gentiles were never called His brethren], ye have done it unto me" (Matt. 25:40, KJV).

4. Christians are to support Israel because it brings the blessings of God to them personally.

In Psalm 122:6, King David commands all Christians, "Pray for the peace of Jerusalem: may they prosper who love you." The scriptural principle of personal prosperity is tied to blessing Israel and the city of Jerusalem.

Why did Jesus Christ go to the house of Cornelius in Capernaum and heal his servant who was ready to die? Jesus went because the Gentile centurion deserved the blessing of God because he had demonstrated his love for the Jews by building a synagogue in Israel (Luke 7:5). When you do things to bless the Jewish people and the State of Israel, God will bless you.

Why did God the Father select the house of Cornelius in Caesarea to be the first Gentile house in Israel to receive the gospel? The answer is given repeatedly in Acts 10.

Acts 10:2 says: "…a devout man [Cornelius] and one who feared God with all his household, who gave alms generously to the people, and prayed to God always." Who were the people to whom Cornelius gave these alms? They were the Jewish people who lived around him.

Acts 10:4 states: "Your prayers and your alms have come up for a memorial before God."

Acts 10:31 reads: "…your alms are remembered in the sight of God."

The point is made three times in the same chapter. A righteous Gentile who expressed his unconditional love for the Jewish people in a practical manner was divinely selected by heaven to be the first Gentile house to receive the gospel of salvation and the first to receive the outpouring of the Holy Spirit.

These combined Scriptures verify that prosperity (Gen. 12:3; Ps. 122:6), divine healing (Luke 7:1–5), and the outpouring of the Holy Spirit (Acts 10) came first to Gentiles who blessed the Jewish people and the nation of Israel in a practical manner. Paul expands on this teaching in Romans 15:27.

The Bible principle for Gentiles being blessed for blessing the Jewish people could be seen with Jacob and Laban. Jacob, one of the patriarchs, worked for Laban, who was a Syrian. Laban changed Jacob's wages ten times, each time to his hurt. Jacob became weary with the abuse and told Laban he was leaving. Laban responded apologetically: "Please stay…for I have learned by experience that the LORD has blessed me for your sake" (Gen. 30:27). Laban was a Gentile who confessed that he recognized God's specific blessing to him and his family because of Jacob.

The blessing continues in the story of Joseph and Pharaoh. Joseph saved the Gentile world from starvation through his divine power to interpret dreams. Pharaoh blessed Joseph by making him the prime minister of the nation and by giving to his family the rich farmlands of Goshen, which were the best in Egypt. Pharaoh treated Joseph and the Jewish people as an extension of his own family. During this era in Egypt's history, the pyramids were built and the glory of Egypt reached its absolute pinnacle. Through the genius of Joseph, the food in storage was used to buy vast amounts of real estate for Pharaoh and Egypt.

Then there arose a pharaoh who did not know Joseph. That pharaoh persecuted the Jewish people. He made their lives grievous and difficult on purpose. The Jews were forced to make bricks without straw. They were beaten with whips, they were starved, and their male children were drowned in the Nile River.

God brought to that pharaoh and his administration ten plagues that destroyed the economy of the nation. In its finality, the firstborn in every Egyptian home died, and the pharaoh himself became bloated fish food, floating facedown before the Jewish people who had been liberated from Egypt's bondage by walking through the Red Sea on dry ground.

It is to be noted that what a nation does to the Jewish people, God will do exactly the same to them. The Egyptians killed Jewish children in the Nile River. God sent a plague that killed the firstborn of every house in

Egypt without the lamb's blood on the door. The tears of the Egyptians matched every Jewish tear to the last drop.

When I went to West Berlin in 1984 as a guest of the US military to speak in their annual week of spiritual renewal, I was taken by a German tour guide through Checkpoint Charlie into East Berlin. What a contrast between capitalism and Communism. West Berlin was an oasis of boundless abundance created by the risk-and-reward system of capitalism. East Berlin was a barren desert with nothing to offer but empty promises. East Berlin was a poster child for Communism.

Separating East and West Germany were two ten-foot-high barbed-wire fences with a no-man's-land of one hundred yards filled with machine gun towers and German shepherd attack dogs. The German tour guide turned to me and fired a question I did not see coming: "Pastor Hagee, why did God allow the Russians to build fences around the German people, with machine guns and attack dogs?"

The answer flashed out of my mouth like lightening: "God allowed the Russians to build barbed-wire fences around the German people to hold you as prisoners with machine guns and German shepherd attack dogs because the German people did exactly the same thing to the Jews at every death camp. You did this at Dachau and

Auschwitz, and for every Jew who died, you will have to answer to God."

5. God judges the Gentiles for their abuse of the Jews.

In Exodus 17, there's the story of the Amalekites, who attacked the children of Israel as they came up out of Egypt en route to the Promised Land. Because the Amalekites, who were descendants of Esau, whom God hated, attacked the Jewish people, God promised to be at war with Amalek from generation to generation.

> Then the LORD said to Moses, "Write this for a memorial in the book and recount it in the hearing of Joshua, that I will utterly blot out the remembrance of Amalek from under heaven." And Moses built an altar and called its name The-Lord-Is-My-Banner; for he said, "Because the LORD has sworn: the LORD will have war with Amalek from generation to generation."
>
> —EXODUS 17:14–16

Because Amalek attacked the Jewish people as they came up out of Egypt, God promised to be at war with him until He drove his remembrance from beneath the sun. That meant God intended to exterminate him and his people. Hundreds of years later, God was still at war with Amalek. God commanded King Saul to destroy the Amalekites utterly. We read:

> Thus says the LORD of hosts: "I will punish Amalek for what he did to Israel, how he ambushed him on the way when he came up from Egypt. Now go and attack Amalek, and utterly destroy all that they have, and do not spare them. But kill both man and woman, infant and nursing child, ox and sheep, camel and donkey."
>
> —1 SAMUEL 15:2–3

In 1 Samuel 15:28, because Saul refused to obey the Lord, God took the kingdom from him and gave it to another. The judgment on Saul was instantaneous, because he refused to carry out God's judgment against those who had attacked the Jewish people.

In 1 Samuel 15:28–29, Samuel said to Saul: "The LORD has torn the kingdom of Israel from you today, and has given it to a neighbor of yours [David], who is better than you. And also the Strength of Israel will not lie nor relent. For He is not a man, that He should relent."

There is a point here that cannot be missed. Hundreds of years passed from the time of Moses to King Saul, but God did not change His mind about exterminating

Amalek's descendants to the last "man and woman, infant and nursing child."

Another illustration of God judging the Gentiles who attacked the Jewish people was the pharaoh "that knew not Joseph."

A third illustration of God destroying Gentiles who attacked the Jewish people is that of Haman. Haman was an Old Testament Hitler who planned the first "final solution" for all the Jews living in Persia. The story is vividly recorded in the pages of God's Word. (See the Book of Esther.) The end result was that Haman and his seven sons hung from the gallows they built to hang the Jews of Persia upon. The judgment of God came to those who tried to bring destruction to the Jewish people. Exactly what Haman planned for the Jews happened to himself and his sons.

Where is the Roman Empire? Where are the Greeks? Where are the Babylonians? Where are the Turks? Where is the Ottoman Empire? Where are Adolf Hitler and his goose-stepping Nazis? They are all footnotes in the boneyard of human history, because they all made a common mistake. They attacked the Jewish people, and God Almighty brought them to nothing.

Hitler had Jews shot and thrown in death ditches and then burned. Others were gassed and burned in ovens, and their ashes filled the countryside like flakes of falling snow. How did Hitler die? He shot himself and ordered his fanatical lunatic Nazi followers to soak his body with fifty gallons of gas and then burn him to an ash. What you do to the Jews will happen to you.

God promises to punish the nations that come against Israel (Gen. 12:3). America, the Arabs, the European Union, the United Nations, Russia, China—indeed, all nations—are in the valley of decision. Every nation that presumes to interfere with God's plan for Israel, including the United States, stands not only against Israel but also ultimately against God. God is rising to judge the nations of the world based on their treatment of the State of Israel.

In March 2002, when White House rhetoric was moving against Israel, Senator James Inhofe (R-OK) gave one of the greatest speeches ever given on the floor of the United States Senate. Senator Inhofe titled his speech, "Seven Reasons Why Israel Is Entitled to the Land."[3]

The key points in Senator Inhofe's speech are shown below:

1. The archaeological evidence says it's Israel's land.

2. Israel has a historic right to the land.

3. Israel's practical value to the Middle East

4. Israel's land: the ground of humanitarian concern

5. Israel is a strategic ally of the United States.

6. Israel is a roadblock to terrorism.

7. We must support Israel's right to the land because God said so!*

---

* This chapter is taken from chapter 20, "Five Bible Reasons Christians Should Support Israel," in *Jerusalem Countdown*.

CHAPTER 8

ARMAGEDDON—BATTLE FOR WORLD SUPREMACY

W HEN RUSSIA AND its allies march into Israel, they will be expecting to march out in victory. There will be no indication to them of what awaits them. They will have no awareness that they are making that march into Israel because God has put "hooks into [their] jaws," or that He is the one leading their armies, "all splendidly clothed, a great company with bucklers and shields, all of them handling swords" (Ezek. 38:4).

Yet in Ezekiel 39, God has revealed the outcome of that confrontation with Israel, telling His prophet what He will do to Russia and its allies when they invade Israel in the near future:

> And I will turn thee back, and leave but the sixth
> part of thee, and will cause thee to come up from
> the north parts, and will bring thee upon the
> mountains of Israel.
>
> —Ezekiel 39:2, KJV

God declares He will exterminate all but one-sixth of the Russian axis of evil that invades Israel. Five out of six warriors in that great army will be killed. That's a death rate of 82 percent within just a few hours. It's no wonder the world will be stricken with shock and awe.

God continues with His strategy of war by saying:

> Then I will knock the bow out of your left hand,
> and cause the arrows to fall out of your right hand.
> You shall fall upon the mountains of Israel, you and
> all your troops and the peoples who are with you;
> I will give you to birds of prey of every sort and to
> the beasts of the field to be devoured.... And I will
> send fire on Magog [Russia] and on those who live
> in security in the coastlands. Then shall they know
> that I am the Lord.
>
> —Ezekiel 39:3–4, 6

This last verse suggests that judgment is coming not only to the invading Russian force but also on the headquarters of that power and upon all who support it or allowed this attack on Israel.

Notice the words: "I will send fire…upon those who live in security in the coastlands." The word translated *coastlands* or *isle* in the Hebrew is *'iy*. The word was used by the ancients in the sense of *continents* today. It designated the great Gentile civilizations across the seas, which were usually settled most densely along the coast-lands—just like America.

This fire Ezekiel sees coming to those living securely in the coastlands could be a direct judgment from God by hurricanes and tsunamis, or it could describe a nuclear war via an exchange of nuclear missiles. Could it be that America, who refuses to defend Israel from the Russian invasion, will experience nuclear warfare on our East and West Coasts? That's exactly where most of us live today.

Why would God allow this? The Bible gives a clear answer: "I will bless those who bless you, and I will curse him who curses you" (Gen. 12:3).

Right now in America's major universities, professors, many whose positions are funded by Saudi Arabian oil money, blast Israel as the cancer on the soul of humanity. In his book *The Case for Israel*, Alan Dershowitz cites how pro-Israel speakers are being uninvited from

America's universities, who boast of freedom of speech.[1] Anti-Semitism is alive and well in America.

Major American denominations are defunding Israel by refusing to buy the stock of any company or corporation doing business with Israel. It is self-righteous for Americans to point their fingers at the atheistic history of Russian and the Islamic fanatics—when we ourselves are not without sin toward the Jewish people and Israel.

How extensive will the judgment of God be upon the Russian-invading coalition? Ezekiel 39:9 states it will take Israel seven years to collect and burn the weapons of war brought into Israel by the invaders.

How many dead will there be? According to Ezekiel 39:11–12, the physical death is going to be so massive it will take every able-bodied man in Israel seven months to bury the dead. Those traveling in Israel from north to south have to travel "stopping their noses" because of the horrific stench from the bodies of the enemies of Israel destroyed by the mighty right hand of God.

WHERE IS ARMAGEDDON?

Many times I have stood on the very ground in Israel that will one day soon be covered with blood drained from the veins of the armies of the world.

As beautifully explained by our tour guide for

twenty-five years, Mishi Neubach, *Har-Magedon* means "the Mount of Megiddo." One can stand at Megiddo and look across the Jezreel Valley as far as your eye can see.

In 1799, Napoleon stood at Megiddo before the battle that thwarted his attempt to conquer the East and rebuild the Roman Empire. Contemplating the enormous plain of Armageddon, the marshal declared, "All the armies of the world could maneuver their forces on this vast plain."[2]

In the Old Testament, this valley is called "the Valley of Jehoshaphat." Joel says, "I will also gather all nations, and bring them down to the Valley of Jehoshaphat" (Joel 3:2). Joel then describes the Battle of Armageddon:

> Proclaim this among the nations:
> "Prepare for war!
> Wake up the mighty men,
> Let all the men of war draw near,
> Let them come up.
> Beat your plowshares into swords
> And your pruning hooks into spears;
> Let the weak say, 'I am strong.'"
> Assemble and come, all you nations,
> And gather together all around.
> Cause Your mighty ones to go down there, O
>   LORD.

"Let the nations be wakened, and come up to the
   Valley of Jehoshaphat;
For there I will sit to judge all the surrounding
   nations.
Put in the sickle, for the harvest is ripe.
Come, go down;
For the winepress is full,
The vats overflow—
For their wickedness is great."

—JOEL 3:9–13

In the Book of Revelation, John the Revelator declared that blood will flow up to the bridle of a horse for a space of sixteen hundred furlongs, which is approximately two hundred miles (Rev. 14:20). It will be a sea of human blood!

Look at a map of Israel. From the northern part of Israel to the southern point is about two hundred miles. The message? The battlefield will cover the nation of Israel!

It is beyond human comprehension to envision a sea of human blood drained from the veins of those who have followed Satan's plan to try to exterminate the Jewish people and prevent Jesus Christ from returning to Earth. Yet, in the theater of your mind, try to imagine the armies of the world, armed to the teeth, representing hundreds of millions of men eager to slaughter each other.

As this great battle begins, the king of the East and the king of the West have gathered in Israel to fight for control of Planet Earth. Just then, the unexpected happens.

THE WAR OF THE WORLDS

Before these great armies can prepare their weapons for assault, there is an unexpected invasion such as Planet Earth has never seen before.

It is not an invasion from the north, the south, the east, or the west. This invasion is from heaven itself. John describes this great invasion with these words:

> Now I saw heaven opened, and behold, a white horse. And He who sat on him was called Faithful and True, and in righteousness He judges and makes war. His eyes were like a flame of fire, and on His head were many crowns. He had a name written that no one knew except Himself. He was clothed with a robe dipped in blood, and His name is called The Word of God. And the armies in heaven, clothed in fine linen, white and clean, followed Him on white horses. Now out of His mouth goes a sharp sword, that with it He should strike the nations. And He Himself will rule them with

a rod of iron. He Himself treads the winepress of
the fierceness and wrath of Almighty God. And He
has on His robe and on His thigh a name written:
KING OF KINGS AND LORD OF LORDS.

—REVELATION 19:11–16

Instantly the Antichrist and the king of the East forget
their hostilities toward each other. In verse 19, John the
Revelator says that the Antichrist and his armies "gathered together to make war against Him who sat on the
horse and against His army." It will be Jesus Christ of
Nazareth who sits upon the white horse.

In this great battle, the King of kings and Lord of lords
captures the Antichrist and the false prophet and casts
them alive into the lake of fire burning with brimstone.

Read what happens next: "And the rest [hundreds of
millions] were killed with the sword which proceeded
from the mouth of Him who sat on the horse. And all
the birds were filled with their flesh" (v. 21).

We stand on the brink of the best of times and the
worst of times. It is the worst because man's rebelling
against God and His purpose for Israel makes it necessary for God to crush Israel's enemies.

Behold, He who keeps Israel
Shall neither slumber nor sleep.

—PSALM 121:4

Just before us is a nuclear countdown with Iran, followed by Ezekiel's war, and then the final battle—the Battle of Armageddon. The end of the world as we know it is rapidly approaching. Yet, through it all, God promises, "All Israel will be saved" (Rom. 11:26).

David's Son, King Jesus, will rule and reign for one thousand years in the Golden Age of Peace from Jerusalem. Rejoice and be exceedingly glad—the best is yet to be.

Notes

Chapter 2
Birth Pains of the New Age

1. PBS.org, "The Iranian Hostage Crisis," *American Experience*, http://www.pbs.org/wgbh/americanexperience/features/general-article/carter-hostage-crisis/ (accessed June 9, 2011).

2. USA-Presidents.org, "James Earl Carter Jr. (1977–1981): Biography," http://usa-presidents.org/james-earl-carter-jr-1977-1981-biography (accessed June 9, 2011).

3. ArlingtonCemetery.net, "Terrorist Bombing of the Marine Barracks, Beirut, Lebanon," October 23, 2008, http://www.arlingtoncemetery.net/terror.htm (accessed June 9, 2011). Israel Ministry of Foreign Affairs, "The Second Lebanon War (2006)," July 12, 2006, http://www.mfa.gov.il/MFA/Terrorism-+Obstacle+to+Peace/Terrorism+from+Lebanon-+Hizbullah/Hizbullah+attack+in+northern+Israel+and+Israels+response+12-Jul-2006.htm (accessed June 9, 2011).

4. About.com: American History, "Fast Facts: Terrorism…World Trade Center Bombing, 1993," http://americanhistory.about.com/library/fastfacts/blffterrorism8.htm (accessed June 9, 2011). Laurie Mylroie, "The World Trade Center Bomb: Who Is Ramzi Yousef? And Why It Matters," *The National Interest*, Winter 1995/96, viewed at http://www.fas.org/irp/world/iraq/956-tni.htm (accessed June 9, 2011).

5. Matt Pyeatt, "Clinton Paid 'Lip Service' to Terror Attacks, Expert Charges," December 6, 2001, NewsMax.com, http://

archive.newsmax.com/archives/articles/2001/12/5/142108
.shtml (accessed June 9, 2011).

6. Ibid.

7. September11News.com, "September 11, 2001—the Day
    the World Changed," http://www.september11news.com
    (accessed June 9, 2011).

8. Ibid.

9. Ibid.

10. Ibid.

11. BBC News Online, "7 July Bombings: Overview," http://
    news.bbc.co.uk/2/shared/spl/hi/uk/05/london_blasts/
    what_happened/html/ (accessed June 9, 2011).

12. Andy Soltis, "Brit 'Baby Bomb' Beasts—Plot to Blow Up
    Own Child and Jet," *New York Post,* August 16, 2006,
    http://nypost.com/seven/08162006/news/ worldnews/brit_
    baby_bomb_beasts_worldnews_andy_soltis.htm (accessed
    October 3, 2006). Posted on *Free Republic* (blog), August
    16, 2006, by PajamaTruthMafia, http://www.freerepublic
    .com/focus/f-news/1684658/posts (accessed June 9, 2011).

13. John Kay and Simon Hughes, "Hunt On for Baby
    Bombers," *The Sun,* viewed at FrontPageMag.com, http://
    archive.frontpagemag.com/readArticle.aspx?ARTID=3089
    (accessed June 9, 2011).

14. Jodie T. Allen, "The French-Muslim Connection,"
    PewResearch.org, August 17, 2006, http://pewresearch.org/
    pubs/50/the-french-muslim-connection (accessed June 9,
    2011).

15. Doug Struck, "17 Suspected Terrorists Arrested in
    Canada," *Washington Post*, June 3, 2006, http://www
    .washingtonpost.com/wp-srv/content/article/2006/06/03/
    canadaterror3.html (accessed June 9, 2011).

16. BBC News Online, "Spain Threatens Iraq Troop Pull-Out," March 15, 2004, http://news.bbc.co.uk/2/hi/europe/3512144.stm (accessed June 9, 2011).

17. F. William Engdahl, "China Lays Down Gauntlet in Energy War," *Asia Times Online,* December 21, 2005, http://www.atimes.com/atimes/China/GL21Ad01.html (accessed June 9, 2011).

18. FOX News and Associated Press, "North Korea, Nations Respond to Possible Sanctions for Nuke Test," October 10, 2006, http://www.foxnews.com/story/0,2933,218699,00.html (accessed June 9, 2011).

CHAPTER 3
ENTER: THE KING OF THE NORTH

1. International Standard Bible Encyclopaedia, Electronic Database 1996, Biblesoft, s.v. "chief."

2. Wilhelm Gesenius, *A Hebrew and English Lexicon of the Old Testament*, trans. Edward Robinson (n.p.: Crocker and Brewster, 1844.).

3. John Cumming, *The Destiny of Nations* (London: Hurst & Blackette, 1864).

4. Hal Lindsey, *The Late Great Planet Earth* (Grand Rapids, MI: Zondervan, 1970), 59.

5. J. Vernon McGee, *Through the Bible,* vol. 3 (Nashville, TN: Thomas Nelson Publishers, 1982), 513.

6. Ibid., 513–514.

7. Gesenius, *A Hebrew and English Lexicon of the Old Testament*.

CHAPTER 4
RUSSIA'S SUPPORTING CAST

1. Ariel Farrar-Wellman, "Russia-Iran Foreign Relations," IranTracker.org, August 2, 2010, http://www.irantracker.org/foreign-relations/russia-iran-foreign-relations (accessed June 9, 2011).

2. Ibid.

3. IsraelSeen.com, "Fact Sheet Russia-Israel Relations," July 30, 2010, http://israelseen.com/2010/07/30/fact-sheet-russia-israel-relations/ (accessed June 9, 2011).

4. Reuters News Service, "Iran Offers Atomic Know-How to Islamic States," *Free Republic* (blog), September 15, 2005, http://www.freerepublic.com/focus/f-news/1484885/posts (accessed June 9, 2011).

5. Ryan Mauro, "Paul Williams Details 'American Hiroshima,'" *WorldNetDaily*, September 3, 2005, http://www.worldnetdaily.com/news/article.asp?ARTICLE_ID=46127 (accessed June 9, 2011).

6. Amy Kellogg, "Nuclear Watchdog Chief Warns of Nukes Falling Into the Wrong Hands," FOXNews.com, January 27, 2011, http://www.foxnews.com/world/2011/01/27/nuclear-watchdog-chief-warns-trafficking-illicit-materials/#ixzz1Dowdj48Q (accessed June 9, 2011).

7. Ibid.

8. Melanie D. Dameron, "Focus of the Nuclear Summit 2010 to Keep Weapons Out of Terrorists' Hands," AssociatedContent.com, April 13, 2010, http://www.associatedcontent.com/article/2887936/focus_of_the_nuclear_summit_2010_to.html?cat=9 (accessed June 9, 2011).

9. Mauro, "Paul Williams Details 'American Hiroshima.'"

10. Ibid.

11. Ibid.
12. Ibid.
13. WND.com, "Nuclear War-Fear: Ayatollah Warns U.S. Needs Punch in Mouth," *WorldNetDaily*, May 1, 2005, http://www.wnd.com/news/article.asp?ARTICLE_ID=44067 (accessed June 9, 2011).
14. Ibid.
15. Joseph Farah, "Iran Plans to Knock Out U.S. With 1 Nuclear Bomb," from Joseph Farah's *G2 Bulletin*, *WorldNetDaily*, April 25, 2005, http://www.wnd.com/news/article.asp?ARTICLE_ID=43956 (accessed June 9, 2011).
16. Joseph Farah, "What Katrina Taught Iran," *G2 Bulletin*, September 19, 2005, 1–5.
17. Farah, "Iran Plans to Knock Out U.S. With 1 Nuclear Bomb."
18. Peter S. Goodman, "Big Shift in China's Oil Policy," *Washington Post*, July 13, 2005, http://www.washington post.com/wp-dyn/content/article/2005/07/12/AR2005071201546_pf.html (accessed June 9, 2011).

CHAPTER 5
AMERICA—TOO LATE, TOO LITTLE?

1. Kim R. Holmes and James Carafano, "Defining the Obama Doctrine, Its Pitfalls, and How to Avoid Them," The Heritage Foundation, September 1, 2010, http://www.heritage.org/Research/Reports/2010/08/Defining-the-Obama-Doctrine-Its-Pitfalls-and-How-to-Avoid-Them (accessed June 9, 2011).
2. James Carafano, "Obama Doctrine Is Failing in the Middle East," *The Foundry* (blog), The Heritage Foundation, http://blog.heritage.org/2011/01/29/

obama-doctrine-is-failing-in-the-middle-east/ (accessed June 10, 2011).

CHAPTER 7
WHY CHRISTIANS SHOULD SUPPORT ISRAEL

1. The Royal Grant to Abraham map was taken from Clarence Larkin, *Dispensational Truth* (Adrian, MI: Lifeline Books, 1918), available now from Rev. Clarence Larkin Estate at http://www.larkinestate.com/index.html.
2. This quote is attributed to Oscar Hammerstein II, who gave it as advice to Mary Martin.
3. "Seven Reasons Why Israel Is Entitled to the Land," given by James Inhofe on March 4, 2002, can be accessed at http://christianactionforisrael.org/inhofe.html (accessed June 10, 2011).

CHAPTER 8
ARMAGEDDON—BATTLE FOR WORLD SUPREMACY

1. Alan Dershowitz, *The Case for Israel* (Hoboken, NJ: John Wiley and Sons, 2004).
2. Philologos.org, "Armageddon," http://philologos.org/bpr/files/a005.htm (accessed June 10, 2011).

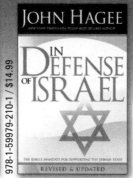
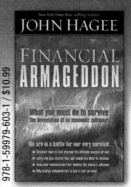

FREE NEWSLETTERS
TO HELP EMPOWER YOUR LIFE

Why subscribe today?

- ☐ **DELIVERED DIRECTLY TO YOU.** All you have to do is open your inbox and read.

- ☐ **EXCLUSIVE CONTENT.** We cover the news overlooked by the mainstream press.

- ☐ **STAY CURRENT.** Find the latest court rulings, revivals, and cultural trends.

- ☐ **UPDATE OTHERS.** Easy to forward to friends and family with the click of your mouse.

CHOOSE THE E-NEWSLETTER THAT INTERESTS YOU MOST:

- · Christian news
- · Daily devotionals
- · Spiritual empowerment
- · And much, much more

SIGN UP AT: **http://freenewsletters.charismamag.com**

8178